Making Invisible
Histories Visible

June L. Mazer (*right*) and Bunny MacCulloch

The June L. Mazer Lesbian Archives

Making Invisible Histories Visible

A Resource Guide
to the Collections

Edited by
Kathleen A. McHugh,
Brenda Johnson-Grau,
and Ben Raphael Sher

UCLA Center for the Study of Women
Los Angeles, 2014

COVER PHOTOS: *Top left:* Diane Germain, circa 1958-59, Diane Germain Papers; *center:* March against Briggs Initiative, 1978, Lesbian Schoolworker Records*; top right:* Motorcyclist at Gay Pride Parade, San Francisco, circa 1980s, photo by Francesca Roccaforte, Francesca Roccaforte Papers; *bottom left:* Rita Charette, 1958, Bunny McCulloch Papers; *bottom right:* Margaret A. Porter and friend, 1935, Margaret A. Porter Papers

—

June L. Mazer Lesbian Archives : making invisible histories visible : a resource guide to the collections / edited by Kathleen A. McHugh, Brenda Johnson-Grau, and Ben Raphael Sher. -- Los Angeles : UCLA Center for the Study of Women, 2014.

128 pages : illustrations (some color)

1. June L. Mazer Lesbian Archives -- Archives. 2. June L. Mazer Lesbian Archives – History. 3. Lesbians – California -- Archival resources. 4. Lesbianism -- Archival resources. 5. Lesbian community — History -- Archival resources. 6. Lesbians' writings -- Archival resources. 7. Lesbian activists -- Archival resources. 8. Women's music — History -- Archival resources. I. Title. II. McHugh, Kathleen Anne. III. Johnson-Grau, Brenda. IV. Sher, Ben Raphael. V. June L. Mazer Lesbian Archives. VI. University of California, Los Angeles. Center for the Study of Women.

HQ75.6.U52 C24 2014 (Z7164.H74 J86 2014)

ISBN 978-0-615-99084-2

—

UCLA Center for the Study of Women
Box 957222/1500 Public Affairs
Los Angeles, CA 90095-7222
310 825 0590 • csw@csw.ucla.edu • www.csw.ucla.edu

The June L. Mazer Lesbian Archives
626 N. Robertson Blvd.
West Hollywood, CA 90069
310 659 2478 • contact@mazerlesbianarchives.org
www.mazerlesbianarchives.org

UCLA Library

Department of Special Collections
Box 951575, A1713 Charles E. Young Research Library
Los Angeles, CA 90095-1575
310 825 4988 • www.library.ucla.edu/special-collections/home

Digital Collections
digital2.library.ucla.edu

Contents

Women's Pentagon Action, Washington, DC, 1981. *Elaine Mikels Papers*

PART II: COLLECTIONS OF
THE JUNE L. MAZER LESBIAN
ARCHIVES

Mack Misstress performing at Sarafemme 2008: Queer Women of Color Music Festival, West Hollywood Park. *Photo by Angela Brinskele. Angela Brinskele Papers*

Preface

The founders of what became the June L. Mazer Lesbian Archives went looking for lesbian history in the early 1980s and could not find it in either the archive or the historical record. So they resolved to gather personal and collective materials themselves in order to make a place for that history. At around the same time, feminist scholars at UCLA founded the Center for the Study of Women (CSW) to make a place for transformative, interdisciplinary research on women as an integral part of the university's mission. In 2007, some two decades later, our missions converged in the partnership we formed for CSW Access Mazer Project. Joined by the UCLA Library, our collaboration flourished and in 2011 the National Endowment for the Humanities provided generous completion funds. Along the way, many people and partners have come together to help realize the vision behind this archival project. This resource book testifies to the important mission of preserving lesbian, feminist history and to the value of community partnership and ongoing collaboration.

– Kathleen A. McHugh
Director, Center for the Study of Women,
University of California, Los Angeles

No matter how carefully considered in advance, there is no way to really know how a new strategic partnership will work out. What a gift the Mazer-UCLA partnership has turned out to be to the Archives, and our grassroots Lesbian community. Almost all our personal collections, plus our video and audio materials, are processed, preserved, and safely stored. While my generation was not as closeted as the generations before, I am old enough to remember the police noting our license plate numbers when we entered the gay center and the librarian going to the locked stacks to get my requested book on "homosexuality." Forty years later it took courage for the Board to decide to trust a large government institution. That courage has been rewarded with mutual understanding and respect, excitement as we discovered the riches in our boxes, and friendship. As I read the graduate student essays I felt their excitement of discovery. What thrilled me most is they were discovering the cares, struggles, successes and joys of everyday, just-trying-to-get-by Lesbians. This is what the Mazer has always been about. This partnership ensures our grassroots Lesbian community will live forever.

– Ann Giagni
President of the Board, June L. Mazer Lesbian Archives

Since being launched in 2009, the outreach and collection-building partnership between the UCLA Library and the June L. Mazer Lesbian Archives has made thousands of documents, photographs, and ephemeral items more broadly accessible, benefiting scholars of social and cultural history around the world. Growing out of a project initiated by the UCLA Center for the Study of Women, this innovative collaboration draws on the strengths of both organizations to support UCLA's mission of teaching, research, and public service. The partnership supports the Library's broader efforts to gather, preserve, interpret, and make accessible collections documenting the remarkable multiplicity of cultures and at-risk hidden histories of the Los Angeles region. We invite scholars to consult the Mazer materials in person or online, and we look forward to our continuing collaboration with both the June L. Mazer Lesbian Archives and the UCLA Center for the Study of Women to continue to expand the pool of primary materials available to researchers.

– Virginia Steel
University Librarian, University of California, Los Angeles

– Sharon E. Farb
Associate University Librarian, University of California, Los Angeles

**March
1959
50¢**

The Ladder

Preserving the Legacy of Lesbian Feminist Activism and Writing in Los Angeles

KATHLEEN A. McHUGH
Director, UCLA Center for the Study of Women

When a Grassroots Organization meets a State Institution

THE JUNE L. MAZER LESBIAN ARCHIVES, located in West Hollywood, California, has collected the papers, images, and ephemera of everyday lesbians since 1981. Originally titled the West Coast Lesbian Collections and founded by Cherie Cox, Lynn Fonfa, and Claire Potter in Oakland, CA, their acquisition policy included "anything a lesbian ever touched." In 1986, June Mazer, her partner, Bunny MacCulloch, and others arranged for the struggling archive to be brought to Los Angeles. "Grassroots" well describes their efforts and the archives that bear June Mazer's name, as the word indicates the groundwork, basis or foundation of something originating in or emerging from people removed or isolated from a major political center.[1] Grassroots archives, to paraphrase Jackie Goldsby, allow us to imagine the histories of people and populations otherwise ignored or left undocumented by the political center.[2] In the Mazer's boxes and materials lie past traces and future imaginings of lesbian and feminist ways of seeing, living, writing, protesting, and, most importantly, desiring and loving. This resource book provides a guide to the Mazer's vital collections while also telling the story of how they came to be housed at UCLA, a large state institution and major research university. Grassroots organizations and state institutions' interests are, by definition, distinct and incommensurate, and the path to this outcome was by no means easy or certain. But it was as necessary as it was groundbreaking.

This book introduces the outcome in two parts. In the first part, short essays from participants in the project address topics that range from the project's history to its legal articulation to the distinct pleasures, insights, and challenges that arise from working with the individual collections. Each essayist has engaged in one or more of the tasks this project entailed: grants writing, fundraising, administering, negotiating, managing, collecting, processing, describing, preserving, digitizing, and housing these collections. The essays in part I convey an archival or institutional materialism; they render the multiple entry points, perspectives, challenges, and solutions that arose within a dynamic collaboration among three separate entities and their respective personnel: the June L. Mazer Lesbian Archives, the UCLA Center for the Study of Women (CSW), and the UCLA Library. These essays introduce the voices of diverse project collaborators whose distinct skills and labors resulted in these collections now being available to scholars and other interested parties around the world, while they maintain their identity and origins in the Mazer Archives.

< *The Ladder,* March, 1959. The first national distributed lesbian magazine in the U.S., it was published by the Daughters of Bilitis until 1970 when the organization disbanded. It was taken over by Barbara Grier, who published it until 1972. *Daughters of Bilitis Records*

Part II presents abstracts of all 83 collections, together with images and representative documents curated by project personnel. Here, readers can sample the range and depth of the collections themselves. The abstracts gesture to the individual lives, the political and social groups and issues, the myriad types of documents and memorabilia, the literature, images, and social documentation produced by lesbians and feminists whose collections are included in this project. This section registers the material value of and the life in these collections, the scholarly opportunities and resources they afford, and the excitement, pleasure, and insight we have all experienced engaging with these materials and bringing this project to fruition. It makes clear why archives–and lesbian archives in particular–matter.

A Bit of History: From "Access Mazer" to "Making Invisible Histories Visible"

IN 2007, CSW commenced what became a substantial and productive relationship with the Mazer archives through a two-year UCLA community partnership grant. Titled "The 'Access Mazer' Project: Organizing and Digitizing the Lesbian Feminist Archive in Los Angeles," the grant provided funds for CSW to process, describe, create finding aids for and digitize five large L.A.–based Mazer collections. Since I became its director in 2005, CSW had implemented a community-based research focus on sexuality, gender, and women in Los Angeles. In 2006, Candace Moore, a CSW Graduate Student Researcher (GSR), now an Assistant Professor at the University of Michigan, suggested the Mazer Archives, where she had conducted dissertation research, as a possible community partner. I did a site visit, met Mazer Board Chair Ann Giagni and board member Angela Brinskele, among others, who agreed to work with us. The Community Partnership Grant we received the following year covered five major collections: the Connexxus/Centro de Mujeres; Women Against Violence Against Women (WAVAW); the Lillian Faderman collection: the Margaret Cruikshank collection; and the Southern California Women for Understanding (SCWU). From this collaboration, the Mazer benefited in having these materials processed and CSW and the UCLA library benefited by having these materials digitally available for scholars worldwide through the California Digital Library.

Martha Foster.
Martha Foster Papers

Though the community partnerships grant included only CSW and the Mazer Archives, the UCLA Library supported us from the start. The grant costs covered digitization equipment and the highly skilled GSRs we employed–James Hixon, T-Kay Sangwand, Janine Liebert, and Adrienne Posner–to process, create finding aids for, and digitize the collections. We divided up the grant's two years by processing the material collections the first year and digitizing them the second. I remember well a conversation I had with Stephen Davison, the head of the UCLA Digital Library Program, as we planned the digitizing process of the five collections. He said, "It is a little irregular for us to digitize collections that the UCLA Library doesn't own." This irregularity–that involved questions of stewardship for the Mazer and concerns about costs and investment for UCLA library–led to negotiations that resulted in a longtime formal partnership between the UCLA Library and the Mazer Archives, negotiations facilitated by CSW.

Couple attending Sarafemme 2008: Queer Women
of Color Music Festival, West Hollywood Park.
Photo by Angela Brinskele. Angela Brinskele Papers

The expanse and state-of-the-art archive facilities at UCLA interested the Mazer, whose collecting activities had been slowed by lack of physical space at their archive; the UCLA Library saw the Mazer as crucial to their "Collecting Los Angeles" initiative and their interest in LGBT Archives and materials. However, the interests of each diverged on crucial points. While the Mazer sought, primarily, to preserve lesbian history for lesbians, with access an important but secondary goal, the UCLA library wanted to enhance their overall collections profile through access. Articulating a successful partnership between the Mazer, a small grassroots organization and UCLA, a large state institution, depended on resolving significant issues concerning collection ownership and stewardship. The Mazer did not want to cede ownership of the collections to an institution that, though currently benevolent, might change their priorities and values in ways detrimental to lesbian history and its preservation. For the library, ownership was a crucial element of investment and public mission. How could they justify an investment of space and resources to these collections if their stewardship rested with parties outside the university who could then remove them from the UCLA library at any time they chose?

Both the Mazer and UCLA needed to be creative to establish a framework for what had not been done before, to change existing policies and procedures and then contractually to modify the existing documents that defined the relationship between the two entities. Though such a partnership had not been legally executed and engaged in before, it was worth the effort for both. The partnership ultimately effected by the June L. Mazer Lesbian Archives and the UCLA Library has to do with the way in which sexuality as well as other differences such as race, ethnicity, and gender, have been structured out of our major social institutions and the work it takes to create a framework that can allow for this work to be included. The essayists in this resource book did the work it took to create this legal framework and to implement the productive collaboration and partnership that followed from it.

The success of our collaboration then led to the NEH awarding us a three-year Humanities Collections and Reference Resources (HCRR) Grant to process, describe, create finding aids for and digitize 83 Mazer collections and a substantial portion of their AV materials. Essays from Ann Giagni, the head of the Mazer Board, and Sharon Farb, UCLA Associate Librarian, recount the details–the problems and the legal resolutions–that initially thwarted and then enabled this partnership. We are also delighted to have an essay from our former NEH program officer, Elizabeth Joffrion, on collaborations between mainstream and community archives that engages multiple perspectives, including lesbian archivist theorists and the NEH program guidelines. These initial essays provide an overarching context for those written by other project participants, from managers to archivists to processors. We began the project in May 2011 and completed it in June 2014.

Acknowledgments: Many Hands

THE EXTENT AND AMBITION of the "Making Invisible Histories Visible" project required numerous and diverse participants, many of who write of their project experience in the essays below. Dr. Julie K. Childers, former CSW Assistant Director, helped write the NEH grant and managed the project for its first two years before relocating to Philadelphia. She served as the point person for all the different units working on the grant. Since her departure, Dr. Pamela Crespin, current CSW Assistant Director, has ably taken up the project manager position. Financial manager Van Do-Nguyen has overseen all the project finances. CSW Publications Manager Brenda Johnson-Grau has, in addition to helping with the grant proposal and doing all the publicity for the NEH project, worked with Ben Raphael Sher and me on editing this resource publication. She curated the images and produced a magnificent layout to illustrate the essays and collection descriptions.

MP Rita Charette enforces the no-men policy, 1958.
Bunny McCulloch Papers

Angela Brinskele, our liaison at the Mazer, served as project consultant and rights permissions manager, tracking down donors, necessary deeds and permissions, planning workshops, doing oral histories, and curating images for this publication. Lizette Guerra, Chicano Studies Research Center (CSRC) librarian and archivist, served as the project archivist; she trained and supervised the many GSRs who processed the collections under her direction. Both she and CSRC Project Archivist Michael Stone, who oversaw all of the Mazer's audiovisual digitizing, previously had worked on their center's LGBT initiative. UCLA Librarian Gary Strong and Library Director of Special Collections Tom Hyry regularly consulted on the project while associate librarians Kelly Wolfe Bachli and Jillian Cuellar have assisted us in organizing the collection acquisition and cataloging. They trained the GSRs and directed all the processing done through the Center for Primary Research Training (CFPRT). Jain Fletcher, rare books cataloger, created bibliographic MARC records for all of the collections. Senior analyst and library liaison Leslie McMichael assisted Sharon Farb and everyone else, facilitating project meetings. Stephen Davison, mentioned above, has continued to guide the project's digitization and access component. Siobhan Hagan helped to establish the protocols for digitization and preservation. And, librarian Diana King served as a steadfast ally and consultant.

The "grassroots" of the project–the hands that have sorted, foldered and scanned documents, drafted finding aids, done interviews, written blogs, and engaged and presented on the collections–are the GSRs we have hired from the Departments of English, Film, Television and Digital Media (FTVDM), History, Information Studies (IS), Moving Image Archive Studies (MIAS), Sociology, and World Arts and Cultures (WAC). Trained by CSW, UCLA Library, and CSRC personnel, the graduate students we selected brought passionate scholarly and personal investments to the project. Kimberlee Granholm (MIAS), who, over the course of the project, completed her master's degree and became a staff member at CSW, worked closely with Angela Brinskele on permissions, processed collections, and is now part of the core team overseeing everything in the grant's final year. Stacy Wood (IS) coordinated with the Mazer, processed and described collections, trained other GSRs and conducted a group oral history with the Mazer Board members. Jonathan Cohn (FTVDM) and Sadie Menchen (MIAS) took up residence at the Mazer as we prepared for digitization, drawing up a detailed list of collections and audiovisual material we proposed to process. Jonathan then digitized audiovisual materials. Ben Raphael Sher (FTVDM) wrote blog posts on the project, processed and digitized a number of collections, and serves as co-editor of this resource book. Daniel Williford (English) worked with Kimberlee Granholm on media digitization. Marika Cifor (IS) has processed collections at CFPRT and has completed an oral history with Ann Giagni as well as other Mazer donor and board members. Angel Diaz (IS), who has particular interests in Mexican American community archives, processed and scanned several collections as did Molly Jacobs (Sociology) whose dissertation has drawn from research she did on the materials for this project.

Director/Producer J.D. Disalvatore (left) with friend at Outfest. Photo by Angela Brinskele. Angela Brinskele Papers

A number of graduate students worked on Mazer collections through the CFPRT: Sandra Brasda (History) processed the Broomstick Magazine records; Gloria Gonzalez (IS) the Margaret A. Porter Papers; Courtney Dean (IS) the Diana Press Records and the Barbara Grier Periodical Collection; and Pallavi Sriram (WAC) the Pat Nordell Papers and others. Last but not least, Jorge B. Lopez helped with processing, Archna

Flyer for a presentation by Diane Germain about lesbian life for family and friends of lesbians and gays. *Diane Germain Papers*

Slide Show about LESBIANS

what are they like ? how are they alike ? what do they like ?

how can we like them even better than before ?

FOR PARENTS AND FRIENDS OF LESBIANS AND GAYS

 by diane f. germain, m.s.w.,

Tuesday September 25th at 7:00 p.m.
at the First Unitarian Church in Hillcrest

corner of Front and Arbor, three blocks North of Washington Street, across from the UCSD Medical Center

Patel worked tirelessly on digitizing collections and doing an overall materials audit, and Sally Marquez and Hannah Caps have helped to create the metadata and descriptive material for the project's oral history collections. All of these efforts help ensure maximum accuracy and access to the processed collections.

We worked closely with a terrific NEH Project Advisory Board: Susan Anderson, Eric Avila, Marie Cartier, Ann Cvetkovich, Lillian Faderman, Ann Giagni, Joseph R. Hawkins, and R. Bradley Sears. Ann Cvetkovich's brilliant writings on the lesbian archive have been an inspiration as has been Mazer donor and historian Lillian Faderman's work, especially *Gay L.A.*, which was invaluable as we conceived and moved forward on "Making Invisible Histories Visible."[3] Thanks to Joseph Hawkins for sharing the ONE Archive's NEH grant proposal that provided a model for ours and to Brad Sears and Eric Avila, colleagues and friends, for their scholarship and activism on LGBT and Los Angeles issues. We are thrilled to have an oral history from Mazer donor Marie Cartier and thank Susan Anderson for all her assistance through the UCLA library.

This resource book provides a summary of all the collections of the June L. Mazer Lesbian Archives that are now available through the UCLA Library. It also makes visible the voices, negotiations, labor, and personnel behind what was an extraordinarily successful, indeed joyful, collaboration among a large and diverse number of people. Thanks to Chon Noriega for suggesting the idea of a resource book. I am deeply grateful to Ann Giagni for her trust and commitment to our longstanding partnership and to Sharon Farb, who brought to it passion, wit, and the legal wisdom necessary to write the contract on which our collaboration depended. Last but not least, my heartfelt thanks to the CSW staff and the wonderful graduate students on whose work the project outcomes ultimately relied. In helping to preserve and provide access to the history contained in the Mazer Archives, we all have, in some small way, become a part of that history.

NOTES

1. *American Heritage Dictionary*, New York: Houghton Mifflin Co, 1973: 574-5.
2. Jackie Goldsby, "The Art of Being Difficult: The Turn to Abstraction in African American Poetry and Painting During the 1940s and '50s." UCLA, Public Talk, February 13, 2014.
3. See Cvetkovich's "Queer Archival Futures: Case Study Los Angeles," in a special issue of *E-MISFERICA*, On the Subject of the Archives, ed. Marianne Hirsch and Diana Taylor, 9.1-9.2, and Faderman and Stuart Timmons' *Gay L.A.: A History of Sexual Outlaws, Power Politics, and Lipstick Lesbians*, New York: Basic Books, 2006.

Wall of History at June L. Mazer Lesbian Archives. *Angela Brinskele Papers*

a safe place for everyday, just-trying-to-get-by Lesbians

ANN GIAGNI

President of the Board, June L. Mazer Lesbian Archives

BEGUN AS A COLLECTIVE THIRTY YEARS AGO, the June L. Mazer Lesbian Archives is a grassroots nonprofit organization. Up until 2007, all work–seeking and acquiring materials; processing and providing access; organizing dances, readings, panel discussions, and exhibits; producing concerts; designing and maintaining the website; and writing grants and managing office and administrative responsibilities–was done by volunteers. Although now one Board member has a 20-hour-per-week contract, the essential grassroots volunteer character of the group has not changed.

Like the collections of other such archives, our materials were scattered. Some were in our public space in West Hollywood. The rest filled two garages and newly arrived materials had spilled into a third garage. We kept urging lesbians to donate materials and they did, but we were out of space. Lack of space and environmental controls forced us to not pursue several important donors. The Board recognized that to grow and thrive we needed to find a different way of doing business.

Out of the blue, the UCLA Center for the Study of Women (CSW) invited the Mazer to be a community partner in a project proposal. We accepted, and the getting-acquainted process began. About a year later, I told CSW Director Kathleen McHugh that I would like to explore a deposit relationship with the UCLA Library, modeled after the relationship the Library had with Outfest. Materials would be stored and preserved by UCLA but the Mazer Archives would retain ownership.

Kathleen arranged a meeting, which included myself, two other board members, Kathleen, then-University Librarian Gary Strong, Associate University Librarian Sharon Farb, and other library and CSW staff members, to discuss the possibilities. Gary indicated that the library could no longer agree to a deposit relationship for several reasons. Because of its mission as a research library (as well as an unpleasant experience with heirs who reclaimed a large collection on deposit and sold it on eBay), materials needed to remain available for researchers at UCLA and public dollars could only be spent on processing and preserving materials owned by the Library. In retrospect, we all agreed that each left that first meeting thinking that it would never fly. It did fly–so what happened?

In the collections of the Mazer Archives are materials that document everyday lesbian life.

The Mazer Archives wanted the relationship with UCLA for clear reasons: space in our existing facility could be freed up and materials could be processed, stored in a protective environment, and made available for public access. However, we recoiled at

PART I: ESSAYS

19

DON'T AGONIZE: ORGANIZE!

(213) 658-8350

JOIN **WAVAW** WOMEN AGAINST VIOLENCE AGAINST WOMEN

"Don't Agonize, Organize" flyer. *Women Against Violence Against Women Collection.*

the idea of giving ownership of Mazer materials to UCLA. We feared that the materials would disappear, be removed from the Los Angeles area (because the Regents can place materials on any campus in the UC system), or left unprocessed and unavailable. Remarkably, once we outlined the reasons for not giving Mazer materials to UCLA, a possible solution presented itself. I called it an "almost irrevocable trust." As we developed a new proposal, the Mazer had an organizational identity crisis. If we give our materials to UCLA, why should anyone give them to us first? Why not go right to UCLA? And if we are not working with the materials donated to us, what will we do?

After much angst, we realized that our great strength is that the Mazer is a grassroots organization with a long history in the community. We routinely collect material from everyday, just-trying-to-get-by, lesbians. We are committed to reaching out to other lesbians who are engaged with grassroots communities and showing them that their lives have historical importance. Many are surprised to hear our message. We believe that if we don't preserve our collective grassroots history, the only information available in a hundred or more years will be newspaper articles, books on celebrity lesbians, and other published material. The rest of us will have vanished. UCLA cannot do this work. They can bring in existing private collections, but they do not have the contacts or the ability to develop contacts within the lesbian community that we do. We now have a clear vision of the role of the Mazer Archives in providing a safe interface between lesbian materials from the grassroots community and UCLA.

In addition, we realized that when a lesbian donates to us and we in turn donate to UCLA, we have the ability to reclaim ownership if the Regents do not abide by the agreement–which provides a reason for donating to the Archives and not directly to UCLA. The Board regularly checks to make sure materials are processed within a reasonable time and kept available in Los Angeles. If they are not, we have the legal right to take them back. Once the Board of the Mazer Archives could see what we could become, we structured a proposal that eventually became the Deed of Gift between the June L. Mazer Lesbian Archives and UCLA.

Our relationship with UCLA has been exciting. We have received a number of major donations because of it. We now feel confident asking for more material because we know there is a safe place for it. An unexpected benefit was CSW's NEH grant to process many of all our holdings. Together with UCLA we are exploring other ways to ensure future historians will have a rich body of love letters, home videos, journals, and organizational papers of small local groups to capture and communicate the lesbian life of those of us who are not rich and famous.

March against Briggs Initiative. *Lesbian Schoolworkers Records*

TAKE PRIDE LESBIAN VISIBILITY

Flyer from Lesbian Visibility Week.
Lesbian Visibility Week Records

Putting the "L" in Collecting Los Angeles

SHARON E. FARB
Associate University Librarian, UCLA

but I give you
a legacy of doers
of people who take risks
to chisel the crack wider.
Take strength that you may
wage a long battle.
Take pride that you can never
stand small.
Take the range that you can
Never settle for less.

– Pat Parker,
Legacy. Jonestown
and Madness, 1985

THE UCLA LIBRARY has fostered an innovative project that gathers, preserves, interprets, and makes accessible collections documenting at-risk and hidden collections of personal histories and cultural artifacts of the Los Angeles region. Thanks to a generous gift from the Arcadia Fund, "Collecting Los Angeles" enables the Library to support civic engagement and to make discoverable previously hidden voices, communities, and cultures that reflect the rich diversity of Los Angeles. The collection encompasses a broad range of material, which includes the Sleepy Lagoon Defense Committee, Garry South Campaign Papers, June Wayne Papers, Aldous Huxley, Paul Monett, Anais Nin, Walter Gordon, Jr/William C. Beverly, Miriam Matthews, A. Quincy Jones, and now the June L. Mazer Lesbian Archives to name a few.

The epigraph by Pat Parker, lesbian, activist, and poet, accurately describes the tireless commitment of the June L. Mazer Lesbian Archives to preserve and document the previously inaccessible voices of everyday and not-so-everyday lesbians, in order to make them accessible for present and future generations. The collaboration between UCLA and the Mazer supports the mission of higher education, furthering new areas of teaching, research, and public service. This collaboration is also integral to the Library's mission of organizing, preserving, and making knowledge accessible in support of the academic endeavor.

In 2009, the UCLA Library, the UCLA Center for the Study of Women, and the June L. Mazer Lesbian Archives formalized a collection-building and preservation partnership that significantly expands access to collections held by the Mazer Archives and enriches the library's holdings in the important areas of lesbian and feminist social and cultural history. Working closely with the Mazer, a long-term Los Angeles–based grassroots lesbian organization, helped the Library develop a model set of agreements, which we continue to use today. These include a collaboration agreement, a model deed of gift and set of mission-critical principles that frame and guide our work together. In this essay, I will describe the importance of the model agreements and highlight several terms and clauses that ensure the sustainability and future of the Mazer Archives.

Mission-Critical Requirements

AFTER a series of meetings between the UCLA Library and members of the Board of the Mazer, organized by Kathleen McHugh, Director of the UCLA Center for Study of Women, we came to an historic agreement to collaborate on the

preservation and accessibility of lesbian feminist history. The Library addressed five essential conditions as put forth by the Board of the Mazer. These requirements assured that the Mazer would continue as a leader in the documentation and preservation of lesbian history and culture. This partnership with the UCLA Library provides the Mazer with safe spaces for collections to grow, an opportunity to organize and preserve these collections in a sustainable way, and to keep the collections open and accessible in Los Angeles. Below is a brief discussion of the five requirements reflected in the clauses included in the Deed of Gift we developed.

Safe Space for Collections to Grow

IT WAS IMPERATIVE that the Mazer continue to steward and grow their lesbian feminist collections. The Mazer had outgrown the space that had been generously provided by the City of West Hollywood. Moreover, that space lacked proper archival climate control and was not properly equipped for fire suppression. The UCLA Library maintains some of the most prestigious manuscript, book, and ephemera collections in the world. The Library has built state-of-the-art secure, climate-controlled environments for these collections, and employs professionally trained archivists, metadata specialists, and digital developers. The partnership between the Mazer and the Library would make sure that the Mazer collection could grow, be made fully accessible, and be preserved for current and future generations. The mission alignment between the Mazer and UCLA Library on this requirement was accomplished by this clause, which describes the UCLA Library's commitment to providing safe spaces for the Mazer collections to grow and flourish:

> The Materials will be physically stabilized and preserved by the UCLA Library including, as appropriate, placing the materials in non-damaging containers and storing in facilities that provide appropriate temperature and humidity control and security. (Paragraph 11: Deed of Gift)

Materials Will Be Available for Researchers

THE JUNE L. MAZER LESBIAN ARCHIVES is a grassroots, community-based collection that relies on volunteer staff to provide access to materials. The UCLA Library's special collections are accessible to the public six days per week. Housing the Mazer Collection at the Library would significantly increase accessibility of the material. The following clause was developed to reflect the Mazer's commitment to accessibility for research:

> The Materials will be available to researchers after they have been arranged and described for use. The Library will create a persistent link to the finding aid and The Materials from the collection that are digitized and will share the link(s) with the June L. Mazer Lesbian Archives so that the Mazer may use on their website or in other venues to advertise the existence of the collection. (Paragraph 12: Deed of Gift)

Collections Stay Together

from left to right, Mona Kindig, Pat Nordell, and Mary Briggs, Mission Ranch. *Photo by John Williams. Pat Nordell Papers*

THE UCLA LIBRARY worked closely with the Mazer from the outset to ensure that we were keeping the best interests of both organizations in mind. One of the five requirements of the partnership addresses the Board's concern regarding the integrity and preservation of the collections, both individually and collectively. The Mazer Board wanted formal assurance that no items in the collections at UCLA would ever be deaccessioned without UCLA providing notice and the right of first refusal.

Right of First Refusal

THE RIGHT OF FIRST REFUSAL was of critical importance to the Mazer and its Board, as it would ensure the integrity of their collections while housed at UCLA. This clause, as added to the agreement, requires that the Library provide appropriate notice regarding any proposed deaccessioning of material to a donor designee of the Mazer. This excerpt details the right of first refusal clause as included in the Deed of Gift:

> In the event that The REGENTS desires to sell, transfer, or assign The Materials, The REGENTS shall send to the DONOR notice in writing of its desire or intention to sell, transfer or assign The Materials. (Paragraph 10: Deed of Gift)

Open to the Public and Located in Los Angeles

ANOTHER of the five objectives of our collaborative agreement guarantees that the Mazer collections will always be accessible to the public, specifically in the city of Los Angeles. UCLA is a large, public university, one of ten campuses of the University of California. The Library remains open six to seven days per week when classes are in session.

In addition, UCLA is a registered not-for-profit educational institution. The following clause was developed under consultation with UCLA Campus Counsel, and received special Regental approval. This language completely assures that the collection would be returned to the donor if UCLA fails to provide unfettered access to researchers regardless of their affiliation:

Books about lesbianism, sexuality, feminism, and activism in chains.
Photo by Francesca Roccaforte.
Francesca Roccaforte Papers

> The Parties agree that if The Materials do not remain accessible to the public at the Los Angeles Campus such inaccessibility (following notice and opportunity to cure) would result in rendering the purpose of the gift "impossible" and shall constitute grounds for return of the entire gift pursuant to applicable Regental policy and standing order 100.4 (v), and pursuant to the standard procedures, including consultation with the General Counsel in accordance with Regents Standing Order 100.4, the gift shall be returned to the donor upon donor's request. (Paragraph 14: Deed of Gift)

In addition to the five requirements addressed in the UCLA Library-June L. Mazer Deed of Gift discussed above, UCLA and the Mazer also developed and agreed to a Collaboration Agreement that helped frame how we would work together. Three key terms in this agreement include the provision that both parties seek collaborative opportunities for grant funding (which we have successfully done), conduct periodic meetings (which we continue to do) and use the "June L. Mazer Archives" to provide appropriate provenance and attribution to the materials entrusted to UCLA. This is an excerpt from the agreement:

> The University of California, Los Angeles (UCLA) Library and the June L. Mazer Lesbian Archive are linked by common interests and seek to develop collaborations in fields of shared interest and expertise. The activities undertaken pursuant to this Memorandum of Understanding (MOU) are based on a spirit of cooperation and reciprocity that is intended to be of mutual benefit to both parties. (UCLA Library/June L. Mazer Lesbian Archive MOU)

The set of discussions leading up to the creation of the Collaboration Agreement and Deed of Gift helped frame and enable what constitutes a highly successful partnership between the June L. Mazer Lesbian Archives and the UCLA Library. In addition, these documents have been used successfully as templates for similar agreements between grassroots, community-based archives and larger institutions. To discover and explore the collections at UCLA, see http://digital2.library.ucla.edu/mazer/.

Celebrate!

The Words of a Woman Who Breathes Fire

KITTY TSUI

poetry & prose

photo by CATHY CADE

MARCH 31, 7:30 **OLD WIVES TALES** 1009 VALENCIA, SAN FRANCISCO
APRIL 19, 7:00 **A WOMAN'S PLACE** 4015 BROADWAY, OAKLAND
APRIL 27, 8:00 **NETWORK COFFEEHOUSE**, 1329 7th AVE, S.F.
with Aaron Shurin, author of THE GRACES

Flyer for *The Words of a Woman Who Breathes Fire.*
Photo of Kitty Tsui by Cathy Cade. Kitty Tsui Papers

The Will to Collaborate

ELIZABETH JOFFRION
Director of Heritage Resources, Western Washington University

MARGINALIZED COMMUNITIES have political interest in the creation, preservation, and curation of documentary material. For many activist organizations, the stewardship of these cultural resources provides verification of a shared history of repression and struggle for civil rights and equal protection. Community archives, such as the June L. Mazer Lesbian Archives, emerge from a collective awareness that limited or biased documentation is an impediment to political activism and that by ensuring an accurate archival record the group can better establish its meaning for members and society at large. This documentation, defined and collected by a community, serves to shape and promote a shared identity that counterbalances their marginalized social status.

Stevens, Flinn, and Shepard (2010) defined community archives "as collections of material gathered primarily by members of a given community and over whose use community members exercise some level of control."[1] In fact, community archives are typically administered by dedicated volunteer activist archivists who recognize the significance of the collections in their care, as well as the importance of a secure community venue for research, discussion, and education. As the collections expand, these untrained volunteers often become overwhelmed by increased research interest and user expectations for reasonable access to underdocumented historical records. To meet these demands, organizations must commit the resources and skills necessary for appropriate access and preservation, including the development of appropriate facilities for archival research and storage. However, the cost of implementing archival best practices and investing in professional development can critically strain already limited internal resources. More importantly, securing the funding required to sustain community archives can conflict with the broader goals and objectives of the organization administering the archive.

It is at this point in their institutional development that many nonprofit community archives first contact a funding agency or mainstream institution to seek advice and assistance. Organizations at this juncture are typically struggling with vital questions related to their vision and strategic priorities. A commitment to long-term professional archival administration essentially expands the organizational mission beyond political activism and social justice to one of service and scholarship. Rather than taking this step, an organization may choose to establish collaborative relationships with outside entities to process or digitize collections, or even to arrange for the transfer of their collections to an established archival repository. This transition can be difficult for many organizations which recognize that mainstream archives have, in some instances, misrepresented,

< Lesbian Midwives and the Gay Nurses Alliance supported Lesbian Schoolworkers in opposing Proposition 6.
Lesbian Schoolworkers Records

neglected, or completely omitted their past from the historical record. And, for many community archives considering these options, there is a fundamental tension between a desire for sustainability and deeply held values of autonomy, independence and self-sufficiency associated with participation in social movements.

Joan Nestle expresses this tension in her work, "The Will to Remember: The Lesbian Herstory Archives of New York."[2]

> In order to survive in America as an archives we have had to call ourselves a not-for-profit information resource centre because the New York State Board of Regents maintains control over educational institutions and could therefore confiscate the collection for 'just cause'. We take no money from the government, believing that such an action would be an exercise in neocolonialism, believing that the society that ruled us out of history should never be relied upon to make it possible for us to exist. All the technology the archives has–the computer, the xeroxing machine–comes from lesbian, gay, feminist and radical funding sources.

Researcher expectations have changed dramatically since Nestle penned these words in 1990. Increasingly, users of archival collections expect access to digitized content, a reality that has only strained the delicate balance between organizational sustainability and mission. Although the availability of online access to collections may reduce staff service obligations, the reality is that developing and maintaining the necessary digital infrastructure is very often beyond the means of most community archives. Many turn to outside organizations for assistance with basic areas of archival practice, including custody, collection development, access, education, and training.

Public funding agencies such as National Endowment for the Humanities, the Institute of Museums Libraries Services, and others, recognize that strategic collaborative partnerships can leverage crucial gains in shared technical infrastructure, staffing and expertise, and provide for more sustainable project outcomes. In fact, most funding agencies now require that applicants address sustainability in their project plans as evidenced in NEH's guidelines for its grant program, Humanities Collections and Reference Resources:

> NEH's Division of Preservation and Access expects that any collections or resources produced in digital form as a result of its awards will be maintained so as to ensure their long-term availability. Discuss plans for meeting this expectation. In addition to pertinent technical specifications requested in the previous section, provide details on digital preservation infrastructure and policies, such as repository system capabilities, storage requirements and capacity, migration or emulation strategies, and collaborative or third-party arrangements, if any.

With NEH support, the UCLA Center for the Study of Women, the June L. Mazer Lesbian Archives, and the UCLA Library entered into a strategic outreach and collection development partnership. Leveraging their shared expertise, staff at these organizations arranged, described, and digitized historically significant papers of lesbian writers and activists; the records of cultural, political, and professional organizations; and oral histories chronicling the lives and personal stories of West Coast lesbian feminist activists. The collections are now permanently housed in the UCLA Library, accessible through their Special Collections and online through the California Digital Library.

Margaret A. Porter (*left*) and fellow members of the Women's Army Corps. *Margaret A. Porter Papers*

Jennie Meyer and Pat Larson.
Photo by Angela Brinskele. Angela Brinskele Papers

Moreover, the relationship with UCLA has inspired the confidence of potential donors and enhanced the collecting efforts of these documentary resources by the Mazer Archives.

The partnership between UCLA and the Mazer Archives was influenced by an earlier NEH award to the ONE Institute's National Gay and Lesbian Archives. Founded in 1952, the ONE Institute houses the largest research library dedicated to Lesbian, Gay, Bisexual, and Transgender history in the U.S., including over 250 archival collections and 2 million items. ONE originated as the earliest national gay publication and evolved into a learning institute that conferred the first academic certificates in gay studies. The ONE Archive, an independent nonprofit organization deposited its collections with the University of Southern California, and now, in return, USC supports a research facility on the campus for the Archive, including building services. In addition, the ONE Archive sponsors campus related events, specialized student research and internships.

These two successful projects provide clear evidence that collaboration between community archives and mainstream institutions has many advantages. Partnerships between two or more organizations can strengthen competiveness for outside funding, offer a means for shared expertise and perspective, and leverage resources to support sustainable infrastructure. And, as noted on the Mazer website, the partnership with UCLA, "makes it possible to ensure that our Lesbian history will be accessible to world."

NOTES

1. Mary Stevens, Andrew Flinn, and Elizabeth Shepherd, "New Frameworks for Community Engagement in the Archives Sector: From Handing Over to Handing On," *International Journal of Heritage Studies* 16 (2010): 59
2. Joan Nestle, "The Will to Remember: The Lesbian Herstory Archives of New York," *Feminist Review* 34 (1990): 92

Marriage Equality booth at Long Beach Pride 2008.
Photo by Angela Brinskele. Angela Brinskele Papers

This is *How We Do* it:

LESBIAN AND FEMINIST ORGANIZING/ORGANIZATIONS

JULIE K. CHILDERS
Project Manager, 2011–2013

THE JUNE L. MAZER LESBIAN ARCHIVES is now well known for preserving the historical record of lesbian lives on the West Coast. Through photographs, journals, letters, oral histories, t-shirts, buttons, and much more, the Mazer Archives aims to assure twenty-first–century lesbians that we are not alone. The "Making Invisible Histories Visible" project makes sure that this legacy is well-maintained and accessible through the unique preservation partnership with the UCLA Center for the Study of Women and the UCLA Library.

While this project spotlights the lives of both remarkable and everyday lesbians, the Mazer is also valuable for the preservation of the record of organized activism found in the papers of local and national lesbian, feminist, and lesbian/feminist organizations. The first collections to be preserved and digitized at UCLA included Southern California Women for Understanding (SCWU), the largest lesbian organization in the U.S. at the time; Connexxus/Centro de Mujeres, which provided services to lesbians in Los Angeles; and Women Against Violence Against Women (WAVAW), which protested violent pornographic media, such as the film *Snuff*. The wave of organizing during the 1970s and 1980s gave rise to many smaller local organizations, as well, both to nurture lesbian community (Los Angeles Women's Community Chorus) and to advocate for the end of discrimination in the workplace (Lesbian Nurses of Los Angeles and Lesbian Schoolworkers)

Feminist and lesbian organizing is beautifully preserved in the organizational records of these groups. Not only do they show the methods and strategies used to pursue change or offer services, but they also reveal, in meeting minutes and correspondence, the internal commitments and debates that shaped the organizations. In a one-line note in the minutes, for example, we learn that the Los Angeles Women's Community Chorus made childcare available at meetings and practices. This community for lesbians was based on common interest (in music and singing), but it maintained commitment to the feminist ideal of access. Because these collections are now available broadly, we can expect a deeper and more complete examination of lesbian and feminist activism during this time.

Given that many of the organizations of the second wave of lesbian and feminist organizing are no longer active, it is important to note that the Mazer Archives is one of the only lesbian organizations still in existence in Los Angeles. Begun in 1981 in Oakland, CA, as the West Coast Lesbian Collections, the Mazer Archives moved to Los Angeles and was renamed after a beloved leader, June Mazer. Likewise, the Center for the Study of Women, which officially opened in 1984, was born of second-wave

August 15, 1978 - Medi-Cal Abortions Cut-Off!

PROTEST MARCH & RALLY

Tuesday, August 15 - Meet at the State Building
107 S. Broadway at 11:30 a.m.
March to the Hall of Administration - 500 W. Temple
for a rally at noon. Protect abortion rights for all women

 NEVER AGAIN  NUNCA MÁS

15 de agosto 1978
¡Fondos de Medi-Cal para abortos han sido anulados!
DEMONSTRACIÓN y MARCHA para protestar

Martes, 15 de agosto - Reunión en Edificio Estatal ("State Building")
107 S. Broadway a 11:30 a.m.
Marcha a "Hall of Administration" - 500 W. Temple por una
demonstración a mediodía para proteger el derecho al aborto
de todas las mujeres.

Por favor distete con ropa negra.   ~   Wear black. ←

Organizada por/sponsored by Reproductive Rights Organizing Committee: 450-2191

STOP BRIGGS
NO ON 6

No on 6 Committee

Santa Barbara Coalition for Human Rights
P.O. Box 770 Goleta, CA 93017

1001 S. Arrowhead Ave.
San Bernardino, Ca.

5106 Wilshire Blvd. L.A. CA 90056

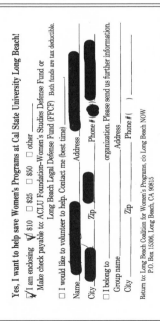

Yes, I want to help save Women's Programs at Cal State University Long Beach!

☑ I am enclosing ☑ $10 ☐ $25 ☐ $50 ☐ other
Make check payable to: ACLU Foundation-Women's Studies Defense Fund or
Long Beach Legal Defense Fund (FFCF). Both funds are tax deductible.
☐ I would like to volunteer to help. Contact me (best time) _____
Name _____ Address _____
City _____ Zip _____ Phone # ( ) _____
☐ I belong to _____
organization. Please send us further information.
Group name _____ Address _____
City _____ Zip _____ Phone # ( ) _____
Return to: Long Beach Coalition for Women's Programs, c/o Long Beach NOW
P.O. Box 15306, Long Beach, CA 90815

34

Woman Power

feminist organizing at UCLA in the late 1970s and early 1980s. The importance of understanding women's lives is at the core of both of these organizations.

In the last thirty years, the political notion that women's and lesbian histories are worthy of documentation has become much less radical. Indeed, that the National Endowment for the Humanities awarded this prestigious grant is a mark of the mainstreaming of feminism and lesbian life in U.S culture. In fact, it marks a particularly mainstream victory. This achievement stands in contrast to what Ann Giagni, President of the Board, identifies as a big political victory for SCWU in its early years: being the first gay or lesbian organization recognized by the IRS as a nonprofit, tax-exempt group with 501(c)(3) status.

As the project manager for this project from May of 2011 to June of 2013 and as a scholar of social movements, I find issues of organization vitally important. I am proud to have been part of this partnership. In the early years of second-wave organizing, the connections between academic feminist groups and community feminist groups were close, the boundaries porous. As the number of activist and community groups declined through the 1990s and as university departments and research centers focused on women's and gender studies became more specialized, these connections frayed. This partnership is a twenty-first–century example of feminist collaboration, an important example of lesbian and feminist organizing in its own right. As we celebrate the work–the preservation and digitization of collections of individual lesbian feminist writers, poets, musicians, soldiers, and activists, as well as the many service and activist organizations they created–made possible by this project, I suggest that we also celebrate this contemporary partnership, which reminds us of the power of building and maintaining organizational alliances.

Margaret A. Porter (*left*) and friend set out to seek their fortunes in
California, 1935. *Margaret A. Porter Papers*

Tracking Down the Deeds

Angela Brinskele

Member of the Board, June L. Mazer Lesbian Archives

LOOKING UP THE DONORS of each collection and asking them to sign the revised deed agreement was one of my responsibilities on the project. Often, this meant that I had to contact people who had donated materials ten, twenty, or even thirty years ago. It was not an easy task and it changed me. I became more organized, learned so much more about the June L. Mazer Archives' collections, and turned into a detective on a mission. Instead of mingling or taking photos, I would stop almost any lesbian at a party and flash them the collection list of names on my phone, asking, "Did you know any of these women?"

So many of the collections now processed contain rich content and great primary source material. For example, the Margaret A. Porter Papers contains about sixty years of personal journals as well as the extensive research that she did on the expatriate women in Paris at the turn of the century. Her thoroughness meant that she contacted libraries in France and family members to get more information and artifacts. For that reason, among the many treasures of her collection are notecards handwritten by Renée Vivian and a book signed by Natalie Barney from around 1910. The collection of Colonel Margarethe Cammermeyer is of great interest. Col. Cammermeyer is the highest ranking officer to be discharged under the U.S. military's "Don't Ask, Don't Tell" policy. Her collection is particularly important because Judge Thomas Zilly of the U.S. District Court for the Western District of Washington ruled that her discharge and the ban on gays and lesbians serving in the military were unconstitutional. Her collection includes her uniform with all her medals placed perfectly. When the uniform was donated, Col. Cammermeyer's wife instructed us, "Don't move anything. It's all measured." Another fascinating and important collection is that of Pat Nordell, a Physical Education teacher and coach at Westchester High School who fought for equal pay for women coaches in the Los Angeles Unified School District. Her collection also contains wonderful photographs including ones of Pat playing on different college and amateur sports teams and a scrapbook featuring her Coach of the Year Award. Other collections feature intriguing materials. The Los Angeles Women's Community Chorus Records, for example, contains some music pages in Braille because at least one member was blind.

All of us at the Mazer are so grateful that these collections have been processed through the hard work of the graduate student researchers at UCLA and the help of Kathleen McHugh, Sharon Farb, and Lizette Guerra. We all hope that this important partnership between the Mazer Archives, CSW, and the UCLA Library will continue to be sustainable so that more materials about the history of lesbians in Los Angeles can be preserved and made available for research.

Yolanda Retter-Vargas (*left*) with Barbara Gittings, UCLA, 2006.
Photo by Angela Brinskele. Angela Brinskele Papers

Collective Imaginaries

LIZETTE GUERRA

Project Archivist

YOLANDA RETTER-VARGAS, my mentor and predecessor at the UCLA Chicano Studies Research Center, taught me that even within my own perceived community there were many communities: Latinas, Chicanas, Lesbianas, feminists, and others. She drilled into my work ethic the notion that I could not truly be at the service of my community, or any community for that matter, if I did not make a true concerted effort to represent everyone, women, men, lesbian, gay, rich and poor, of all cultural backgrounds and beliefs. Yet, historically, this belief has not been central to our profession. Archivists have been privileged with the power to decide what is deemed historical and what is not. What do we preserve for future generations and what do we leave out of our collective imaginaries?

Despite the reality that Los Angeles is one of the most diverse cities in the world, people of color and the LGBT community in particular continue to be underrepresented and in effect invisible within archival collections, the public record, and historical research. The partnership between the UCLA Library, CSW, and the Mazer Archives reflects an increasing awareness amongst archivists and librarians about the importance of collecting more ethnic studies and LGBT materials. In recent years, our profession has been moving away from exclusionary collecting practices and progressing toward more community-oriented approaches that include donors and patrons in the archival process. The collections in the Mazer Archives project not only reflect this nation's rich history, but also, more importantly, provide communities who have long been under-served and under-documented within the historical record with a resource that respectfully reflects their experiences and contributions to U.S. history. Each step of the way, we have made it our priority to include the Mazer Archives' staff and affiliates in the archival process. We have chosen to do so because each of the stories contained within the collections represents a community's memories. The presence of such materials within an institution such as UCLA contributes to a community's visibility, legitimation, and continuity.

"If we don't collect these things," Yolanda always said, "no one else will." The partnership between UCLA and the Mazer Archives is a perfect example of the type of innovative project that Yolanda would have supported. This partnership has allowed us to document and provide wide access to documentation of early lesbian activist and literary history in Los Angeles since the 1930s–stories that might otherwise have been lost or forgotten. As Yolanda wrote in her dissertation, *On the Side of Angels: Lesbian Activism in Los Angeles, 1970-1990* (University of New Mexico, 1999), "Amid the criticisms, let it be remembered that once there was a vibrant movement that put women first. In a world that was (is still) bent on undermining women, that kind of prioritizing and commitment deserves respect and study. Regardless of what terms are used to describe (or disparage) the lesbian activist movement, its spirit persists within the generational cohort that created it during a 'social moment' in U.S. history. It persists as a vision, an ideology, a submerged network and as a significant contribution to the tradition of resistant consciousness and pro-woman advocacy. Blessed Be."

BROOMSTICK

By, For, and About Women Over Forty

Estab. 1978   WINTER (#1) 1991   Price: $5.00

Broomstick was a feminist magazine published between 1978 and 1993 that confronted ageism, stereotypes of the disabled, and gender conventions. *Broomstick Magazine Records*

Processing Papers

Collection Notes by SANDRA BRASDA, COURTNEY DEAN, MOLLY S. JACOBS, ARCHNA PATEL, BEN RAPHAEL SHER, AND STACY WOOD

Broomstick Magazine Records
by *Sandra Brasda*

EXTREMELY REWARDING and instrumental to my academic career, my time processing the collection of *Broomstick Magazine* offered a valuable glimpse into the complex world of library science, archival theory, practice, application, and future problems and possibilities that libraries face. Working on the collection also opened up new areas of inquiry for my own research. And, the knowledge I gained collaborating with other graduate student researchers who were processing materials from the June L. Mazer Lesbian Archives allowed me to discover a rich trove of unmined material perfect for my dissertation research. The materials from the Mazer Archives have become a substantial source base for my dissertation.

An independent, self-published, radical feminist magazine dedicated to supporting and promoting women and lesbian activism and art for an audience of women over forty, Broomstick was founded in 1978 by Maxine Spencer and Polly Taylor in the San Francisco Bay area and ceased publication in 1993. The collection documents the growth of radical feminism in the late 1970s and 1980s and includes materials related to radical feminist politics, lesbian culture and art, spirituality, women and aging, and feminist coalitions and communities. It also contains Spencer's personal papers, documenting her own experiences with radical feminism, lesbianism, disability, sexism, and age discrimination.

The magazine's main goals focused on confronting ageism, stereotypes of the disabled, and gender conventions in publishing. Its specific focus on disabled, lesbian women over 40 adds to the magazine's unique research value: ageism and disability had not been covered extensively at that point in the feminist literature. Because *Broomstick* was specifically focused on women over 40, it is an important resource for those interested in the generation gap between second-wave feminists during the 1970s and 1980s. The records also

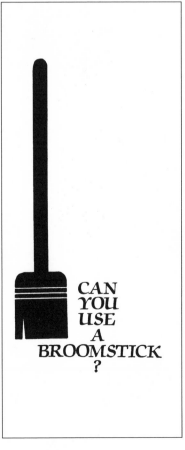

CAN YOU USE A BROOMSTICK ?

Uppity Women Unite!

"Uppity Women Unite!" flyer. *Broomstick Magazine Records*

Making Invisible Histories Visible

provide evidence of the alternative spiritual lifestyle movement active in *Broomstick*'s underground feminist network. The magazine helped establish a spiritual community centered on the venerated image of and faith in the Crone. In addition, the magazine was at the forefront of exploring fat phobia and body consciousness issues.

Broomstick's policy of participatory journalism–its readers provided most of the content–made it stand out from other magazines published during the same period. The magazine's editors actively solicited letters, poems, short stories, and articles. These participatory records–"author files"–make up the majority of the collection. *Broomstick* provided a unique venue for older women to publish their art, poetry, and creative and feminist writing, while building and supporting feminist coalitions and communities. Though it was a small, do-it-yourself publication, it often reached a national and international audience.

History's greatest gift is knowledge, which must be preserved and made accessible for all. As an historian, I found it thrilling to have been able to participate in the operations that go into processing and making available such a significant archive.

Preserving the History of Lesbian/Feminist Periodicals, Publications, and Publishers
by *Courtney Dean*

ARCHIVAL COLLECTIONS containing primary source materials from traditionally silenced or ignored communities are especially compelling to me. Working with materials from the June L. Mazer Lesbian Archives has allowed me to contribute to making previously invisible lesbian/feminist activist and literary histories part of the official archival record.

I had the opportunity to process two separate collections, the first of which was the Barbara Grier Periodical Collection. A lesbian/feminist activist, writer, and publisher, Barbara Grier (1933-2011) is perhaps best known for her work with *The Ladder*, the monthly magazine published by the Daughters of Bilitis, the first national lesbian organization in the U.S. Writing under the pseudonyms Gene Damon, Vern Niven, and Lennox Strong, Grier began contributing copy to *The Ladder* in 1957; she became editor in 1968 and publisher in 1970. In 1973, she co-founded Naiad Books, later Naiad Press, the preeminent lesbian book publisher that opened up lesbian writing to the world. The materials in this collection make up a rich assemblage of feminist and lesbian newspapers, magazines, journals, and small press publications. The bulk of the

A highlight of the Diana Press Records is the assemblage of letters of support from the feminist community following a serious vandalism incident in 1977, including letters such as this one from poet Audre Lorde. *Diana Press Records*

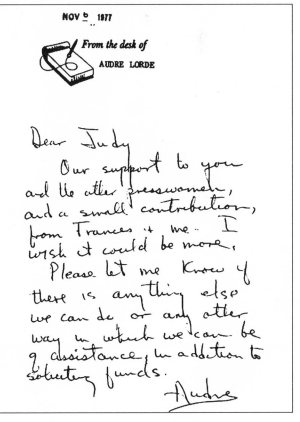

The Ladder

OCTOBER, 1957

material is from the 1980s and features periodicals from major U.S. metropolitan areas as well as small towns, providing snapshots of local communities and individual lives. A particular strength of the collection is its range of formats, including weekly LGBT newspapers such as Pittsburgh's *Out*, newsletters from organizations like Seattle's Lesbian Resource Center, bibliographic resources like the University of Wisconsin's *Feminist Periodicals,* and personal publications such as Dorothy Feola's *Women's Network*.

Following the Grier collection, I processed the Diana Press Records. Diana Press was a lesbian/feminist printing and publishing house started by Coletta Reid and Casey Czarnik in Baltimore, MD, in 1972, which then relocated to Oakland, CA, in 1977. Most notably, Diana Press published titles by writers such as Rita Mae Brown and Judy Grahn, and reprinted Jeannette Foster's pioneering *Sex Variant Women in Literature*. However, the press was also plagued by a series of major misfortunes, including a fire in 1975 and a crippling incident of vandalism in 1977, which destroyed thousands of copies of books and damaged essential printing equipment. Economic setbacks, disagreements amongst leadership, and the dissolution of Coletta and Casey's long-term relationship, led the press to cease publication in the late 1970s.

The records document its storied history through a wealth of administrative materials, author and project files, press and publicity materials, poetry and manuscripts, and a sizeable amount of correspondence. Also included in the materials are assorted newspaper clippings, catalogs and periodicals, and distribution materials and ephemera from community events and organizations. The breadth of correspondence is especially rich, containing both letters to and from the press and documenting everything from requests for catalogs to significant disagreements with authors. A particular highlight of the collection is the assemblage of letters of support from the feminist community following the vandalism incident in 1977, including letters from such feminist luminaries as Adrienne Rich and Audre Lorde. Also notable are the manuscripts that went unpublished for lack of funds. Judy Chicago's *Revelations of the Goddess* appears in the collection in draft and typeset versions.

Both the Barbara Grier Periodical Collection and the Diana Press Records are representative of the diverse, inspiring, complex, passionate, and sometimes messy histories of lesbian and feminist communities. I hope that the collections inspire not only new scholarship but an increased awareness and understanding of the significance of these publishing activities by current and future lesbian/feminist communities.

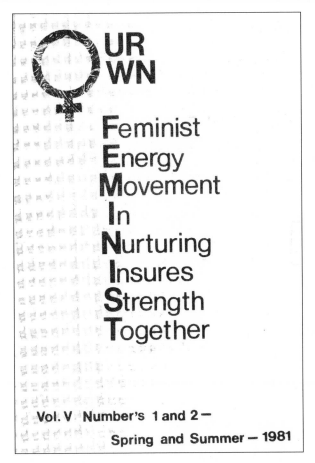

How Do We Know What We Know?
by *Molly S. Jacobs*

I STARTED my work as a graduate student researcher on this project by cataloging two small collections: Joan Robins and the Jewish Feminist Conference. My primary interest, however, was in the Daughters of Bilitis (DOB) Records, because I examine this organization in my dissertation. When I took a precursory glance at the boxes of this collection, I was relieved to see that most of the documents were in file folders with straightforward labels (SF chapter, National Chapter, letters). As I started going through these folders, I soon realized there was much overlap (copies of documents were occasionally filed in several different folders), and some items had been clearly misfiled. I would need to examine each document and set up a new filing system.

The project was overwhelming, and yet it helped me realize two things that are significant for any researcher (or person invested in the preservation of historic documents). First, I was constantly reminded of the process of building knowledge. When discussing methods with my students, I always ask them, "How do we know what we know?" Although I designed the question to get them to think critically about research (and stop referring to sociology as the study of common sense), it became a revelation in terms of how I think about archives. As researchers, we approach an archival collection through its finding aid. Typically, it is organized chronologically and, when it comes to organizations, may be separated by major individuals, chapters, and types of documents. Working on this collection made me ask, "How do I know what I know?" Who decides how these archives are organized? With the DOB, for example, what makes one document a product of the San Francisco Chapter and another the National Chapter? Since both were housed in the same office for some time, how do we know what goes where and how these choices would affect a researcher's understanding of the documents, the collection, and the organization?

Old Lesbians Organizing for Change used images of owls such as this one as a symbol of the wisdom that comes with experience. *Old Lesbians Organizing for Change Records.*

The second realization related to the degree to which researchers become involved with the human side of the archives. As a burgeoning comparative-historical sociologist, I sometimes joke that I do historical research so that I don't have to deal with people. Here in these archives, however, the people are so real. As I worked on cataloging, I should have been able to move more quickly through each mixed-up folder. Instead, as I debated where each document belonged, I became engrossed in the lives of these (mostly) women, presenting themselves through documents from fifty, sixty, even seventy years ago. I tried to spend no more than a few seconds on each document, but doing so was often difficult in terms of understanding where a document fit, or because I wanted to read everything. There was no way for me to give the collection its due without thinking about the people that created it.

These two realizations have continued to resonate for me. I have to think critically about the way that archives are organized and how that affects the way I, and others, use them. Even if an archive box is delivered with files and documents that are labeled and organized down to the smallest minutiae, they were not created that way. Additionally, as we become further removed from the early years of this organization, it becomes more essential to tell their story in a way that retains their humanness, their realness. These women paved the way for great things in this country: for women to organize, to come out, and to see that they weren't alone. By processing all of these collections, the Mazer Archives are preserving the voices of women who wouldn't be silenced in their day and will not be silenced today.

Scanning
by *Archna Patel*

SCANNING. That's what I do. I take a document from a large folder out of an even larger box. I enter its identifying data in an spreadsheet. I push a button, and after a slightly blinding light, voila! It's done! No. It isn't. This process continues for hours, with more folders and more boxes. Doesn't this sound exciting? Well, actually, yes, it is.

Processing and scanning materials for this project has given me the opportunity to think more deeply about the nature of an archive and its value. As an undergraduate, my contact with archives has been quite limited. Yet, the concept of an archive has emerged in several class lectures. One common thread has been the characterization of the archive as a device of control. The archive, the literature says, is a constructed source of knowledge, power, and authority. Rather than being an unfiltered supply of primary material, the archive is an entity that fixes meaning.

One day, I came across a note about the recording of a conversation between two women, Michelle Johnston and Kathi Beall. On the title page was this peculiar sentence: "These women are not famous, they are just two ordinary dykes!!!" "What?" I thought. Not only do the documents record the conversations of these seemingly ordinary lesbian women but the conversations themselves are quite ordinary: What type of music do you like? What did you eat for dinner today? Did you watch *Star Trek* last night? These extraordinary ordinary conversations made me realize that although archives were used and are still used to create so-called official histories of people, places, and periods, they can also become spaces of intervention for people who would otherwise be omitted from the grand narratives of history.

This unexpected sentence made me realize that this was, in fact, the purpose (or at least one of them) of the Mazer Archives: to hold the records, narratives, and experiences of these incredible women whose histories might have otherwise been suppressed or left out of the official history of the late twentieth century. By reading through these seemingly infinite documents, I learned of this wonderfully recent history—the struggle for representation, the struggle against discrimination—and the lives of lesbian women and the organizations they created. Oh, the organizations! Scanning the papers of the National Gay and Lesbian Task Force, Old Lesbians Organizing for Change and others, I realized these documents serve as a testament to the agency of these women and their active participation in their environments.

I also came across memos between the Task Force and the City of West Hollywood discussing the formation of the Mazer Archives. Included was a letter from a constituent who wrote, "The Archives should continue to serve as a living, growing source of positive identity for the community it documents." The Mazer Archives not only preserve the past but constitute a dynamic resource that continues to provoke questions and thereby unfix meaning. I feel fortunate to have played a small role in making this unique resource accessible to more people. Although at times tedious, I know that people from different backgrounds and different places will be able to explore the wealth of knowledge in these scanned documents.

Stories
by *Ben Raphael Sher*

I AM ADDICTED to people's stories, and I believe that one of the great gifts that academics possess is our ability to shine light on the lives, work, and experiences

Martha Foster.
Martha Foster Papers

About Us

Las Hermanas Women's Cultural Center and Coffeehouse is a women's space, organized and run collectively by community women to provide a space for all women to share, learn, and enjoy ourselves together. We, the Las Hermanas workers, are women of mixed racial, ethnic, and class backgrounds. We are workers, students, mothers, mostly (though not exclusively) lesbians and feminists. We believe that women need to organize and work together to become aware of our strengths and struggles worldwide, and to build a consciousness of our shared oppression. We hope that the coffeehouse can contribute to part of this process. Through food, music, films, workshops, and discussion groups we are learning about our class, racial, cultural and lifestyle differences, and are trying to find the common ground that we share as women.

Las Hermanas
Women's Coffeehouse
& Cultural Center

4003 Wabash Avenue   San Diego   280-7510

Fridays 5-11   Saturdays 5-11   Sundays 10-2

of a diversity of people. Because of this, I've felt so lucky to have the opportunity to explore the rich materials in the June L. Mazer Archives from such a variety of angles. I have worked on and off at CSW during the last seven years, and it might be my favorite of the Center's many great research projects. As a graduate student researcher, I have digitized issues of the *Lesbian Catholics Together* newsletter, conducted interviews with Ann Giagni and Angela Brinskele about their life and work, and written blog entries on different collections. The collections I've written about include the papers of the Daughters of Bilitis, and the personal archives of Diane F. Germain, Martha Foster, and Tyger-Womon.

I've been especially struck by the mysterious and even magical qualities that the Mazer Archives take on in their sometimes unpredictable preservation of times, people, and places. For example, Angela Brinskele told me about looking through photos that she'd taken of LGBT events in Los Angeles a decade ago and spotting a person in the background who had been a total stranger, and was now a close friend. Stacy Wood and I tried to solve the mystery of the beautiful and glamorous Martha Foster, who left behind a collection of spectacular photos of herself dressed like a movie star in what appears to be the 1930s and 1940s, with barely any descriptive information.

It felt almost unfair that I got paid to spend several hours drinking coffee with Ann Giagni and hearing about her fascinating life, which intertwined with most of the social contexts and events that affected LGBTQ life in the uniquely dynamic period after World War II. She has seen many not-for-profit organizations come and go

Las Hermanas began as a seven-room collective house for women who were seeking refuge from abusive spouses, and eventually expanded in order to create a safe cultural space for any interested women. The Women's Coffeehouse & Cultural Center opened its doors in 1974 and closed in 1980. *Diane Germain Papers*

About Lesbian Catholics Together*......

11/88

Who We Are:

L. C. T. is a group of Lesbian Catholic women who celebrate home liturgies and paraliturgies together once a month. Most of us have Catholic backgrounds, but some do not. We come together to support each other in whatever ways we can, both spiritually and emotionally. We are attempting to remain committed to the faith in which most of us were raised, rather than depart to other, perhaps more accepting, religions. By doing so, we hope to be a part of that mechanism which will cause change in the Roman Catholic church attitudes and positions on both women and homosexuals, particularly those which suggest that we are psychologically or spiritually diminished.

A Brief History:

The group began informally in the summer of 1986. A small number of longtime women Dignity members, concerned that Dignity was having little success in attracting equal numbers of women to their services, decided to experiment with holding women-only home liturgies. At that time it was felt the overall goal was to introduce women to Dignity. After the first year and after talking with women we had met, we abandoned the goal of direct association with Dignity and decided to continue on our own, resolving, as has Dignity, that we were not a substitute for a woman's regular place of worship. At present, after over two years in existence, we typically find twenty or more women at each liturgy. Many warm friendships have begun, and they continue to develop and grow. We view L.C.T. as still in formation, with the specific purpose of providing a safe and accepting atmosphere in which to socialize, worship and share spiritual journies. Our activities are open to all women, and we are self supporting through optional member contributions.

Recent L. C. T. News:

In 1989 we will begin a celebration of MONTHLY liturgies. Six of these will be home liturgies celebrated with a priest. The remaining six will be para liturgies which will be planned by all of us. We are especially excited about the proposed para liturgies which we hope will provide each of us with an opportunity to share each of our special and unique ideas on worship.

We have been fairly actively involved with the L. A. Gay and Lesbian Religious Coalition this past year. Among their plans for 1989 are an inter-faith service and an inter-faith dance. We will keep you posted on exact dates. In addtion, we would like to remind you that Dignity Long Beach has a women's outreach mass once a month and the phone number for more information can be found on the schedule enclosed.

ATTENTION BISHOP CONATY GRADUATES

Any of you who might have graduated from Bishop Conaty High School in Los Angeles will be interested to know that three studies on the school's future have now been completed --- one on the reconstruction and renovation, one on projected enrollment and one on potential funding for the building expenses. The Archbishop will make the final decision in December after a series of committee meetings, but it now looks like Catholic Education for central and inner city high school girls will continue in Los Angeles. If you would like more information or would like to be involved call (818) 506-8177 and leave a message.

Mailing List Reminder:

This is, really (!), the last mailing you will receive from L.C.T. unless you let us know that you wish to remain on the mailing list. If you have already done so, don't worry, we know who you are! Please take a moment and fill in the small form below and return it to us. And, while you're doing it, tell us what activities you would like in the future. Thanks !

Yes, I wish to continue to receive Notices from L.C.T. _____

Name: _____

Street: _____
City: _____ State: _____
Zip: _____

Mail to: Anita Y.
1828 S. Mansfield Av. L.A. 90019

---

*Member, Los Angeles Gay and Lesbian Religious Coalition

In 1986, Lesbian Catholics Together emerged as an independent entity from the group Dignity USA, an organization founded in 1969 to support and unite gay Catholics, in response to the lack of women at Dignity's services. *Lesbian Catholic Together Records*

throughout her career, and her insights into the elements that have contributed to the organization's longevity would be invaluable to any LGBTQ person hoping to follow in the footsteps of the past and present board members and start a community organization.

In our interview, Ann Giagni said that the Mazer Archives' responsibility is to historicize and preserve documentation of the lives of ordinary lesbians. As a scholar and queer person, I most value this philosophy. The celebration of the lives and work of ordinary lesbians reveals their extraordinariness. If a more normative archive might preserve the papers of a mainstream filmmaker or film studio, the Mazer Archives preserve the papers of a grassroots organization that protested mainstream media representations of women and lesbians and actually forced the entertainment industry to change. If more normative archives preserve the papers of famous published authors, the Mazer Archives also celebrate the work of unpublished poets whose output deserves to be read.

The Mazer Archives comprehensively document the important public work that lesbians have done as activists. However, I think that I love them most for also document- ing the private. In these collections, we see records of real lesbians and feminists grappling with childhood traumas, falling in love with people and pets, serving in the military during the reign of "Don't Ask, Don't Tell," living in women's communities, and collecting potentially offensive lesbian pulp novels which they love nonetheless. The Mazer Archives, as a whole, ever-expanding unit, is among the closest things that we have to a work that represents, with

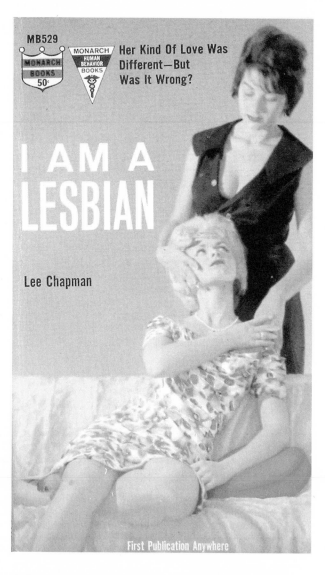

I am a Lesbian, a novel written by Marion Zimmer Bradley under the pseudonym Lee Chapman, was published in 1962. It is one of many pulp novels in the collections of the Mazer Archives.

true comprehensiveness, the day-to-day lives of lesbians and feminists in the twenti- eth and twenty-first centuries. They are so rich and so vast in their documentation of lives and communities that many would still like to see made invisible, that it almost seems as though some extra-human miracle brought them to us. Yet those of us who have watched the development of this project know that the miracles that have made these materials accessible were wrought by the dedicated and hardworking people who gathered, maintained, and processed them. Their work, represented in this book, constitutes another series of inspiring stories that the Mazer Archives tell.

Collective Intimacies
by *Stacy Wood*

OVER THE PAST THREE YEARS I have been fortunate enough to process many individual collections from the Mazer Archives, each taking on its unique contours, representing both an historical moment as well as generously contributing to the collective intimacies of the lesbian archival record. Over time, one begins to rec- ognize that almost every collection contains evidence of community involvement and organizational activities, professional commitments as well as deeply personal materials, evidence of the impossibility of separating or compartmentalizing lesbian lives.

The collection policy of the Mazer Archives has always been generous–"anything a lesbian touches"; its local focus and grassroots history are clear. These collections are

EACH PICTURE
WILL BE,
TO THE LAST
A FLEETING
MOMENT
RESCUED FROM
THE PAST.

SEE ALL YOUR
RELATIONSHIPS
AS SACRED
AND THEY WILL
MIRROR YOUR
SOUL

"Celebrating the Women in My Life, 1915-200?" *(detail),* collage on screen created by Ester Bentley. *Ester Bentley Papers.* *Photo by Angela Brinskele.*

vital snapshots of the history of Los Angeles, bringing social movements into relief in formal and informal manifestations. It is here where we see the indispensability of community archival practices, self-documentation, in telling history on one's own terms, capturing not just the facts of the past but the messiness of their construction.

It is inevitable that while working so closely with materials, you begin to become attached to certain collections, certain relationships, and certain senses of humor that you can glean from personal correspondence. At times, collections seem to be in communication with one another, filling in gaps, serving as connective tissue between seemingly disparate women. Some collections serve as hubs in a wheel, fanning outward to capture not just the movement of a community but the movements of individuals within that community. By collecting materials not tradi-tionally thought of as archival, the Mazer Archives attempts to express and reconstruct everyday life instead of focusing just on the exceptional. T-shirts are alongside financial documents, crafts next to birth certificates.

Many of the collections were deposited informally, friends dropping off boxes, women donating materials for their friends and lovers. As a result, we often may not know much about the donor, able only to use the contents to fill in the gaps. After months of research, reaching out to the community and even making a pilgrimage out to an address contained in a collection, I recognized a mystery donor in the artifact of another. Still housed at the Mazer Archives is a standing screen constructed by Ester Bentley. A collage of photographs, drawings, decorations, and aphorisms, it is titled "Celebrating the Women in My Life, 1915–200?" (Bentley died in 2004). Although I knew from speaking with those active in the Mazer Archives, as well as through my processing work, that the collections represented a networked collective in various states of organization throughout its history, the screen provided a visual understanding of those connections through a single individual's life experiences. This screen captures not only the many connections that were so difficult to find through a paper trail alone but also the impetus behind the Archives. "Each picture will be to the last a fleeting moment rescued from the past" is written on the screen, highlighting the immense amount of love, care, and work that has gone into and will continue to go into these archives.

Part of the Mazer Archives' extensive video collection.
Photo by Angela Brinskele. Mazer Collection of Video Materials

Processing Audiovisual Materials

Collection Notes by JONATHAN COHN, MARIA ANGEL DIAZ,
KIMBERLEE GRANHOLM, MIKE STONE, AND DANIEL WILLIFORD

The Dyke Olympics and Other Lesbian Pastimes
by *Jonathan Cohn*

THE AUDIOVISUAL MATERIALS in the June L. Mazer Lesbian Archives include an assortment of home movies and recordings of speeches, conferences, dances, parades, concerts, fundraisers, socials, retreats, news stories, comedy routines, television episodes, movies, and documentaries. In addition, there are also thousands of prints, slides, and art depicting everything from the making of documentaries to events like gay pride parades, meetings, classes, camps, protests, parties, retreats, and the Dyke Olympics. As a graduate student researcher on the project, I cataloged and began the process of digitizing these materials.

The audiovisual collections of the Mazer Archives offer amazing insights into a wide variety of lesbian and/or feminist communities throughout the 1980s and 1990s. Home videos, photos, and audio recordings illustrate both the everyday lives and influential activism that took place within these communities. While digitizing the audio collection, I listened not only to speeches, lectures, and performances, but also to dozens of social functions ranging from dances to raffles. At these events, anonymous attendees largely discussed their support for one another and pride in their communities. These conversations–along with scrapbooks filled with images of families, celebrations, and travels–illustrate an ethos of compassion, care, and hope often obscured in popular representations of lesbians, gays, and feminists from this period, which tended to focus on AIDS, discrimination, or scandal. While mainstream media represents lesbians always in relation to heterosexuals, the Mazer Archives represent these communities on their own terms.

At the same time, the many recordings of academic and activist conferences depict the complexity

Dyke Olympics, Chapel Hill, NC, 1983. *Photo by Elaine Mikels. Elaine Mikels Papers*

and variety of lesbian identity and feminist praxis. The topics ranged from the history of lesbianism to ecofeminism and the latest in breast cancer research. These conferences demonstrate
not only the impact of lesbian and feminist communities on many current global issues, but
also the many debates and arguments during the period concerning definitions of feminist
theory and how this theory could best be practiced. I became captivated by an administrative
meeting at a conference for Jewish lesbians, which quickly turned into an impassioned debate
over whether or not male children should be allowed to attend panels or the conference's
childcare program. In order to make the conference a safe and open space for lesbians, the
organizers only wanted lesbians to attend. Some in the audience feared that allowing lesbians to bring their sons would make other audience members feel uncomfortable and less
inclined to discuss personal and/or controversial topics. Others feared that by not allowing
sons to attend, those parents who could not afford childcare would be unable to attend.
While grappling with a seemingly small issue, this debate exemplifies the complicated and
always negotiated nature of feminist praxis at every level of life. These small and enduring
moments are also what make the Mazer Archives such an important collection, very much
worth preserving and making available to a larger public.

Witnessing History
by *Maria Angel Diaz*

THE AUDIO COLLECTIONS from the Mazer Archives contain recordings of conferences, workshops, meetings, performances, radio broadcasts, interviews, and
oral histories. These materials concern topics such as homosexuality, lesbian issues,
feminism, racism, discrimination, literature, music, and history from the 1970s through
the 1990s. The bulk of the materials are audiocassette tapes, which were processed and
digitized. Since the digitizing takes place in real-time, it felt like I had almost become a
witness to the events they depicted. As I watched them take place, I developed a deep
understanding of the women, their words and work, their personalities, and the time
and place in which they lived.

A highlight of the materials is a set of interviews from June L. Mazer and Bunny
MacCulloch concerning the Southern California Women for Understanding (SCWU),
Mazer Archives, Mazer's death, and lesbian culture in the San Francisco Bay Area.
Recordings provide great insight into the life and work of both women. The two
interviewed scholars and other experts on lesbian culture and history and were themselves interviewed. The materials also include a recording of the memorial service that
honored the life and work of Mazer after her death in 1987. As an information professional, I particularly enjoyed hearing MacCulloch's description of the organization
of the Mazer Archives, with its details about the collections and the donors, as well as
her nontraditional scheme for organization.

The digitized collections present a range of topics with a variety of hosts and
speakers. From music recordings to scholarly talks to medical information sessions, the
audio materials capture the culture, diversity, politics, scholarship, and activism that
feminist and lesbian communities have produced and engaged with in the U.S. over
the last fifty years. One recording, titled, "Rape City Mall," includes materials from a
project that took place over three weeks in 1977 to raise awareness among Los Angeles
inhabitants of the frequency of assaults against women across their city. The event included speeches, interviews, self-defense demonstrations, and an art piece by Suzanne
Lacy. The recording includes Lacy explaining her intentions in producing the piece
and interviews with the public as they passed by, reacted to, and watched her as she
cited the number of reported rapes that had occurred in three weeks in May of 1977.

Weightlifter at Dyke Olympics, Chapel Hill, NC, 1983.
Photo by Elaine Mikels. Elaine Mikels Papers

The Reading Performances Series (1980–1983) features reading performances by a variety of lesbian and feminist writers, including Eloise Klein Healy, Judy Grahn, Margaret (Peg) Cruikshank, Judy Freespirit, Kent Hyde, and Terri de la Peña. A number of recordings from radio shows include a KPFK presentation about the Stonewall Riots, and the KPFA show Women's Magazine, which featured Del Martin discussing domestic violence within heterosexual and homosexual relationships. Many of the locations where the performances were held no longer exist, making the recordings integral to marking the cultural and historical significance of the sites.

Some were recorded at the Woman's Building, a nonprofit arts and education center founded in 1973 by Judy Chicago, Sheila Levrant de Bretteville, and Arlene Raven. Originally located in MacArthur Park and then on Spring Street, it was a safe space for women to create art, write, collaborate, meet, and develop their senses of identity and community. Although the Woman's Building closed its doors in 1991, it left its mark as a vital base for the feminist movement in Los Angeles. A set of recordings documents the Women Writers series held at the venue. The events in this series were mostly organized by Eloise Klein Healy, a Los Angeles–based poet who published five

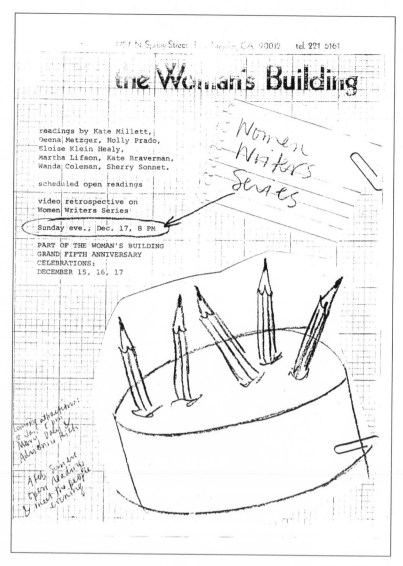

Flyer for "Women Writers Series," which featured Eloise Klein Healy, Wanda Coleman, Holly Prado, and others. Some of the readings are available in the Mazer Collection of Audio Materials. *Woman's Building Records*

books of poetry, founded Arktoi Books, taught at the Woman's Building, and served on its board of directors. She was named Los Angeles Poet Laureate in 2012.

Listening to and describing the ample audio materials of the Mazer Archives has provided me the opportunity to observe quite closely the lives and work of diverse groups of women over the span of several decades. My observations often felt intimate, because many recordings feature small group meetings of women, and sometimes men, sharing personal experiences. As such, they offer a profounder understanding of the atmosphere and sentiment of the time. Before working on this project, I was not well-versed in lesbian and feminist history. I have gained so much from hearing these voices. I not only have learned about the development of lesbian and feminist activism, but I also was fortunate to have helped make available an integral piece of the story of Los Angeles and of California.

To Protect

by *Kimberlee Granholm*

As a graduate student researcher, my assignment involved evaluating and prioritizing the video media for preservation by taking into account each item's uniqueness and relevance to the project's goals; performing repairs; completing digital transfers for preservation and access; rehousing tapes to achieve adequate archival standards; establishing standards for cataloging; and creating descriptions for individual records by researching ideas, events, or persons pictured or referenced within the record.

Often shot using hand-held cameras, most of these tapes were recorded on VHS in the late 1980s to the early 1990s. Since VHS is a fragile medium that begins deterioration after ten years, even when stored in temperature- and humidity-controlled environments (which these were not), these recordings–such significant cultural histories–were in serious danger of extinction, especially since the majority of these tapes were sole existing documents. Given this, I felt that above all, my job was to protect.

The video collection represents an integral aspect of the Mazer Archives: community. While the paper collections mostly focus on individuals, many of the recordings embody a collective identity, albeit one with significantly different opinions. Repeatedly, we see in these videos of group workshops and conference discussions an expressed emphasis on the importance of creating a safe space to disagree. This emphasis was significant: solidarity within the lesbian feminist community was established not by a single opinion but by the collection of individual voices. These groups sought to form a cohesive expression of determined existence, and an identity formed by individuality within the collective. This same ideal is also expressed through the entity of the Mazer Archives.

Watching each tape, I learned to be a better feminist and humanitarian, as well as to be a stronger ally in supporting the Mazer Archives' struggle to keep this history alive. My task was not only to conserve it but also to keep it active and available. Consequently, my selections for priority in digitization and description revolved around assuring an ardent presentation, and thus preservation, of a lesbian feminist heritage within an institutional university, where lesbians can continue to–as the Mazer motto goes–viably "live forever."

A Curse as Blessing
by *Mike Stone*

As a member of the audiovisual processing team, it was my job to oversee the processing of thousands of hours of audiocassettes, videotapes, and Super 8 films. The technology required that the analog materials be digitized in real time. In terms of time management, it may have seemed like a curse but, for an archival project like this, it was actually a blessing. Digitizing in real time is slow and time consuming, but it gave the student staff–all of whom had been chosen because of their special interest in the collections or in related fields of study–the time to listen and to watch, thereby putting their knowledge and skills to work. They could identify materials of historical interest that a casual worker might not have been able to spot. This information could then be added to the metadata, and the finding aid. This collection of descriptive information, more than any special technical innovation inherent in the digitization, is what is most important for a project such as this. It is precisely these notes that add tremendous value and viability for researchers, and will do so for many years to come.

Where Lesbians Live Forever: Video and the Historical Subjects of Lesbian Existence
by *Daniel Williford*

The motto of the Mazer Archives, "Where Lesbians Live Forever," emphatically opposes the effacement of lesbian existence. To build and maintain an archive of lesbian existence was and remains an urgent political act. As I worked on digitizing videotapes for this project, I was struck in particular by the amateur aesthetics, which indicate that home video camera and consumer-grade VHS and Betamax® tapes were used. Set up at a social gathering and left to run for hours, the camera inhabits the sidelines and is often overlooked but what it can record from such a vantage point can be all the more authentic and illuminating.

Following my summer appointment digitizing parts of the video collection, I taught a class at Occidental College's Department of Critical Theory and Social Justice, where I asked undergraduate students to discuss essays by influential lesbian feminists concerning the critical moment in U.S. history when the lived experience of lesbians was articulated as a form of resistance to abusive and oppressive male power. During this discussion, I described my work in archiving some of the video

Woman wears "Psychey Dykey" t-shirt. *Photo by Francesca Roccaforte. Francesca Roccaforte Papers*

materials from the Mazer, which gave an element of currency to the decades-old texts. We discussed Adrienne Rich's statement about how male power works to "deny women [our own] sexuality," which cites as an example "the closing of archives and destruction of documents relating to lesbian existence."[1] She describes how male power has worked to withhold from women "large areas of the society's knowledge and cultural attainments," including "the 'Great Silence' regarding women and particularly lesbian existence in history and culture."[2] Compulsory heterosexuality, according to Rich and Monique Wittig, works in part by making the history of lesbian existence invisible through denial; by describing women's erotic connections as either for reproduction or else as a pathology; and by effacing female traditions. In talking about this project, I was able to show students that such theories were the basis for ongoing efforts to fight back against invisibility, to make sure that lesbians not only "live forever" but have always presented a challenge to the foundational biases of modern society.

Videos capture speakers during meetings and gatherings; others feature candid conversations among attendees of these gatherings. Women discuss their own history and the history of gay and lesbian politics and so capture this oral history, but they also document how community events can facilitate a transfer of knowledge. When lesbians gather together to discuss politics, history, sex, and contemporary lesbian life, the telling of stories and the sharing of experiences not only educates but also insists: lesbians exist and lesbians have always existed. At the Southern California Women for Understanding "Camp Herstory" convention in 1990, for example, panelists–including Ivy Bottini, Robin Tyler, and Donna Smith–were asked "to share with us what in their life has brought them to this point and to show us the history of where the gay and lesbian movement has been in the early part of this century." Smith talks about being young and visiting gay clubs in Hollywood in 1939, including the Lakeshore, where she met her lover. When she says that she and her lover were together for forty years until her death in 1979, the audience applauds and cheers, while Tyler visibly checks her emotion. The audience applauds the existence of a lesbian relationship that lasted through some of the harshest decades in the twentieth century for out lesbians and celebrates the possibility of love in a culture of homophobia.

In a video of the second conference for Old Lesbians in San Francisco on August 5, 1989, Pat Bond does a comedy routine as one of more than a dozen performances recorded. Informally titled "Conversations With Pat Bond," she talks about being a "queer kid" from Davenport, IA, her life in the military, and her experience of gay and lesbian nightlife and activism. Bond tells the story of how she became so infatuated with a professor at San Francisco State College that she took her class over and over until the registrar barred her from enrolling again. During the final exam, Bond says, "I handed in my final blue book with tears in my eyes. And she handed me her phone number." They had an extended, loving romantic affair only because Bond was no longer her student. Bond's story reminds us of the sensual and erotic element of sharing knowledge about lesbian existence and the cathartic effect of shared laughter.

Capturing conversations amongst lesbians who are less well known, the tapes provide glimpses of a broad community of lesbian women. A video of a talent show held at the Los Angeles-based Califia community in 1983 includes a pre-show conversation in which several women discuss aging and motherhood. Discussing how she felt when her children began to have grandchildren, a woman says, "By the time they had kids, something started going to my head, there's something interesting going on here. There are two generations of human beings that have started out in my body." The women speaking with her talk about the need to affirm the success they feel at surviving rather than the fear and regret of losing their youth. Much of the tape documents the talent show, which includes many children, and shows how community education happens through inclusion. In one bit, a woman points the camera at another woman who wears a rainbow "mustache" painted on her upper lip and who giggles with embarrassment at being filmed. "I think if you had a camera pointed at you," she retorts, "you'd find out how embarrassing it is." The point is taken, and the camera is handed over. Blurred treetops and sideways images reveal the transfer while instructions for use are given: "This bottom button goes all the way in, and once you get all the way in, you focus." While the mustached woman figures out how to use the camera, the women she films wave and giggle. She asks one to tell her a story, which descends into gossip about who is sleeping with whom, and for that matter who is a lesbian. "Why wonder when you can ask?" she giggles from behind the lens.

Video materials include recordings of poetry readings, conference panels, comedy presentations, gay pride parades, meetings, classes, camps, protests, parties, and retreats. *Mazer Collection of Video Materials*

The camcorder is passed around and captures a social world in the early 1980s. The materials in the Mazer Archives document not only formal presentations by activists and artists but also lesbian feminist praxis in moments like this one which are all the more poignant for being so mundane.

Against the unchanging forgetfulness of the world, the Mazer Archives insist that we not forget our indebtedness to the lives of lesbians, and that community memory works against the violence of erasure and against the pain of alienation.

NOTES
1. Adrienne Rich, "Compulsory Heterosexuality and Lesbian Existence," *Signs: Journal of Women in Culture and Society* 5: 4 (1980), p. 638.
2. Rich, p. 640.

OWL
Old Wise Lady

OWL (Old Wise Lady). *Drawing by Gloria Churchwoman. Elaine Mikels Papers*

Oral Histories

AS A COMPANION PROJECT TO the processing of the collections, CSW conducted a set of oral histories to preserve the voices of some of the women who have shaped the June L. Mazer Lesbian Archives past and present. The oral histories also add another dimension to archival collections associated with the interviewees. Each of the interviews documents the life of one woman, including childhood; education and employment; activism and politics; family, identity, relationships, and community; and involvement in the Mazer Archives and collaboration with the Center for the Study of Women and the UCLA Library.

Each oral history, which will be available through the UCLA Center for Oral History Research, was conducted over three to five audiorecorded sessions of up to two hours each, which allowed for great depth and breadth. Marika Cifor conducted interviews with Ann Giagni and Marilee France. Angela Brinskele conducted interviews with Marsha Epstein, Jinx Beers, and Judith Saunders. Additionally, the members of the Board of Directors of the Mazer Archives–Ann Giagni, Jeri Deitrick, Marcia Schwemer, Marilee France, Pat Williams, Margaret Smith, Jamey Fitzpatrick, and Angela Brinskele–gathered together in November of 2013 to hold a video group oral history. Filmed by Yvette Soleto and facilitated by Stacy Wood, this oral history documented many aspects of the Mazer Archives' history and activities.

Each of these women offer candid, moving, and original insights in their own powerful words. Together, the oral histories provide a nuanced, diverse, and affecting story of American lesbian and feminist histories and experiences.

Angela Brinskele, who is Director of Communications at the Mazer Archives as well as a member of the Board, conducted several of the oral histories and participated in the group history.

Home
by *Marika Cifor*

// KINDA come clambering up the steps and I walk into the room and it's wall-to-wall lesbians and they're loud, they're raucous, they're laughing, and the room is very, very crowded and I just felt I'd come home. I'd just found where I belonged. It was just this remarkable experience…I think if you have always [had] a place [where] you belong, you don't know what it's like not to have a place where you belong …when you've grown up with this sense of I don't belong here… and then you walk into a room and you think this is it, I knew I was right. I didn't have a place before but now I do."

In the second session of my oral history interview with Ann Giagni, President of the Board of Directors of the June L. Mazer Lesbian Archives, she shared this experi-

Jinx Beers, 1970. *Photo by Wendy Averill. Jinx Beers Papers*

Making Invisible Histories Visible

Wendy Averill (*left*) and
Marilee France and friends.
Photo by Angela Brinskele.
Angela Brinskele Papers

ence, of leaving behind her isolation and loneliness and being welcomed home into the lesbian community for the first time. Ann's insight points to precisely why collecting, preserving, and making accessible lesbian and feminist history is so important. It is so meaningful to do work on this project, because it ensures that no woman who accesses the Mazer Archives will ever feel the same pain of thinking that she is alone.

I have had the opportunity to work on the CSW/Mazer Archives project, and to take the oral histories of two women, Ann Giagni and Marilee France. In their activism with and beyond the Mazer Archives, these women have played profoundly important roles in the making and preserving of lesbian and feminist history. It has been a tremendous and moving experience to hear their stories.

My experiences doing oral histories for this project have revealed the value of lesbian archives as both intellectual and affective experiences. Because doing oral history well requires a great deal of preparatory research, I had the opportunity to delve into the Mazer Archives and gather material from secondary sources on lesbian life, lesbian and feminist activism, and organizations. In spite of all of my preparation, nothing could have prepared me for the actual experience of sitting down to have conversations with these women. Truly collaborative dialogues, each of these oral histories was a self-conscious and disciplined conversation between the narrator and myself. Each allowed me to capture some of the stories, feelings, and meanings and how they were and are still significant to her. Each oral history ultimately illuminates how their individual experiences connect with larger histories.

Ann and Marilee continually provided detailed and fascinating insights into the lived experiences of individual lesbians, their communities, and lesbian and feminist activism in Los Angeles from the 1960s to the present day. Each spoke of experiences ranging from growing up as LGBTQ people, to consciousness raising, to changes they have lived through in the lesbian community. As a scholar of lesbian history and archives, I was surprised at the extent to which their voices brought lesbian and feminist histories to life for me in new ways and moved me deeply. Oral history has a profoundly important role to play in capturing histories that would otherwise be silenced in the archival record. It was a privilege to be part of creating, preserving, and making accessible these lesbian histories.

March opposing Proposition 6 (called the Briggs Initiative after the California legislator who proposed it), which was one of the first attempts to restrict lesbian and gay rights through a ballot measure. It was resoundingly defeated when a coalition—including organizations in the lesbian and gay community, public officials, and conservative, moderate, and liberal groups—mobilized to oppose it. *Lesbian Schoolworker Records*

Making Invisible Histories Visible

Couple attending San Francisco Dyke March, June, 2006. *Photo by Angela Brinskele. Angela Brinskele Papers*

Motorcyclist, San Francisco, circa 1980s. *Photo by Francesca Roccaforte. Francesca Roccaforte Papers*

"What are the Wild Waves Saying?" Try Lesbianism. *Woman's Building Records*

Califia Community, Autumn, 1982. Formed in 1975 and disbanded in 1987, Califia community was a grassroots, feminist alternative education and activist group in Southern California. *Diane Germain Papers*

Attendees at West Coast Women's Music and Comedy Festival, Yosemite, CA, 1985.
Photo by Angela Brinskele. Angela Brinskele Papers

Top left: Dyke March, West Hollywood, 2012; *top right and bottom:* Dyke March, Silver Lake, Los Angeles, June 12, 2005
Opposite: Long Beach Gay and Lesbian Pride Parade, 2012. *Photos by Angela Brinskele.*

BRING
SHARON
HOME

COMMITTEE TO FREE SHARON KOWALSKI

59¢

59¢

59¢

ARE YOU
WILLING TO
DIE FOR
EXXON?

"In Germany they first came for the Communists, and I
didn't speak up because I wasn't a Communist.
Then they came for the Jews, and I didn't speak
up because I wasn't a Jew. Then they came for
the trade unionists, and I didn't speak up
because I wasn't a trade unionist. Then
they came for the Catholics, and I
didn't speak up because I was a
Protestant. Then they came for
me — and by that time
no one was left
to speak up."
—Pastor
Martin
Niemöller

If Logic
Prevailed
Men Would
Ride Side-
Saddle

PRACTICE
RANDOM
KINDNESS &
SENSELESS
ACTS OF
BEAUTY

Let
ME
choose!

AH-SHIT

JOBS
with
PEACE

KEEP
ABORTION
LEGAL

MX

WE CAN'T
HOLD EACH OTHER
WITH
NUCLEAR ARMS

MAY 9 1982, HELENA
MOTHERS DAY VIGIL FOR SURVIVAL

KEEP ABORTION LEGAL

Buttons collected by Diane Germain. *Diane Germain Papers*

LesTalk
The Magazine For Empowering Lesbians/Womyn
FREE! ($1.50 Where Sold)
Vol. 4 No. 12 JUNE 1995

1920: Clear Waters

lesbian connection

Volume 20, Issue 2
September/October 1997

free to lesbians,

but the suggested donation is $4.50/issue
(more if you can, less if you can't)

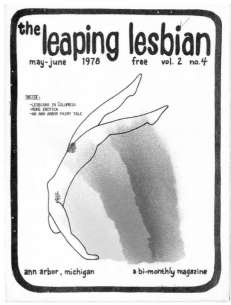

the leaping lesbian

may-june 1978   free   vol. 2 no. 4

INSIDE:
- LESBIANS IN COLUMBIA
- MORE EROTICA
- AN ANN ARBOR FAIRY TALE

ann arbor, michigan   a bi-monthly magazine

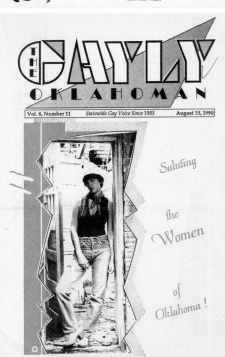

THE GAYLY OKLAHOMAN

Vol. 8, Number 11   Statewide Gay Voice Since 1983   August 15, 1990

Saluting

the

Women

of

Oklahoma !

the Ladder

JUNE   50¢

THE LESBIAN NEWS

Volume 12
Number 4
December 1986

A Digest of Information and Opinion from Southern California and Beyond

Los Angeles

LESBIAN NURSES CHANGE MEETING SCHEDULE

Lesbian Nurses of Los Angeles, a professional organization for RN's in all areas of nursing practice, education and research, has changed its monthly meetings to the last Saturday evening of the month at 5 PM. Meetings are held in the homes of members on a rotating basis, mostly in West LA. The next meeting is on December 6th and will be a "Winter Solstice and Holiday" potluck. Come join a great group of warm and supportive feminist, Lesbian, registered nurses. For more information call Sue at (213) 479-2276, Pat at (213) 484-1298, or Rose at (213) 202-6374. --announcement

MURAL TO RAISE FUNDS FOR PEOPLE WITH AIDS

"Blue Moon Trilogy," a 180-foot long, 30-foot high mural, will be painted at the Odin Street underpass near the Hollywood Bowl in Hollywood to raise funds for AIDS Project Los Angeles (APLA.)

Symbolizing the human transformation that will occur as a result of the AIDS crisis, "Blue Moon Trilogy" will help AIDS Project Los Angeles fund programs which provide assistance to people who have AIDS and AIDS-related illnesses.

Supporters of the AIDS Project Los Angeles are encouraged to purchase inches of the mural for one dollar each. Funds will be contributed through active involvement of corporations and the business community.

" ' Blue Moon Trilogy' is a metaphysical vision, a contemporary version of an ancient art form," said artist Russell Carlton, 24, who will paint the mural. "The bright healing colors in 'Blue Moon Trilogy' represent powerful healing energy that we are all creating in response to the AIDS epidemic."

AIDS Project Los Angeles is a community service organization dedicated to providing vital support and services to people with AIDS, and education to the general community. Staffed by the foremost experts on AIDS and AIDS-related issues, APLA provides more than 30 client support, education and professional training programs. --announcement

RESEARCH PARTICIPANTS WHO ARE INCEST SURVIVORS NEEDED

Volunteer subjects are needed for a two-hour interview concerning their awareness process in psychotherapy. Subjects must be incest survivors. $5 given per interview conducted in geographic location of participant.

If you have been in therapy (individual, group or couple) for at least two months in the past year with a therapist who is not a specialist in working with incest survivors, please call: Dr. Loretta M. Birckhead, RN, EdD, Psychotherapist, Assistant Professor, UCLA, (213) 825-8447. --announcement

FESTIVAL OF LIGHTS

The Church of the Followers of the Great Mother invites you to participate in a celebration of light on Sunday December 14, 1986 at 7 PM.

This spectacular event is held annually at a time when spirits are open to connecting light and energy. Bring your energy; they'll supply the light.

Please call for information and directions. There is no charge. The Church of the Followers of the Great Mother is located at 735 Sunnyhill Drive, Los Angeles, CA 90065; (213) 221-3377. --announcement

RAP GROUP FOR DIFFERENTLY-ABLED LESBIANS

A rap group for differently-abled Lesbians is now forming and will be held at Connexxus, 9054 Santa Monica Blvd., W. Hollywood. If you would like to participate and share some of your views/concerns with other differently-abled Lesbians, please contact Kay at (818) 701-1276. --announcement

CONNEXXUS OPEN HOUSE

Connexxus will have been in operation two full years in January. Joint them and celebrate their presence in the Lesbian community at an Open House on Friday, December 12, from 5-9 PM. Free admission and light refreshments, entertainment. While you are there, be sure to check out the additional 1000+ sq. ft. of space they have just acquired across the hall. Connexxus is located at 9054 Santa Monica Blvd., West Hollywood (between Doheny and Robertson), (213) 659-3960. --announcement

Lesbians of Color, older, differently-abled, or economically disadvantaged women are especially encouraged to submit articles, news releases, columns and calendar events.
NEXT DEADLINE: Copy: December 10, 1986 ; Camera Ready Ads: December 15

BROOMSTICK

BY, FOR, & ABOUT WOMEN OVER FORTY

VOL. VI, NO. 2   MARCH-APRIL 1984 $2.50

LCN News & Views

Volume 1, Issue 6   June, 1991

Wish I was a lesbian so I could go to the picnic.

Hey! Kids are welcome with their moms!

So... which one of you lesbians wants to take me to the LCN Pride picnic?

LCN PRIDE PICNIC
JUNE 23
@ KEY LARGO
11 AM - 9 PM
$6 PER PERSON
KIDS UNDER 12 - FREE

FREE PARKING   CRAFTS   DRINK SPECIALS   GAMES   PRIZES   DUNK TANK
VOLLEYBALL   FOOD   DISCO   ENTERTAINMENT   ARTISTS   VENDORS

Printed on Recycled Paper

The SCWU Newsletter

SOUTHERN CALIFORNIA WOMEN FOR UNDERSTANDING

VOLUME XII, No. 4   AUGUST-SEPTEMBER 1988

Lesbian Agenda Setting

Following the March on Washington, SCWU and NOW sponsored a forum to set a national lesbian rights agenda. Recognizing they could only begin to set up a method for creating such an agenda in that one meeting, they asked NOW's Lesbian Rights Committee to develop a process to achieve that goal.

The result is the National Lesbian Rights Conference to be held October 7-10 at the Holiday Inn at the Embarcadero in San Diego.

While the planning for the Conference continues, there are several issues that are expected to be covered. Those issues include visibility, legal rights, lesbian health care, domestic violence, lesbian families, sexuality, substance abuse, electoral politics, coalition politics, spirituality, being out in the workplace, and lesbians in the arts and media.

The full line-up of speakers has not yet been confirmed, but some headliners include *continued on page 2*

ALSO·IN·THIS·ISSUE

Tell-Tale License Plate 2
Auction 4
Parade Pics 8
New Staff ....10, 16 & 18
Gay Civil Rights 12
Name Our Newsletter 18
1989 Dinner 21
Democratic Convention 22
and lots more . . .

NATIONAL COMING OUT DAY

OUR FIRST National Coming Out Day is Tuesday, October 11, 1988. The date was picked to correspond to the National March on Washington last year, and the debut of the AIDS quilt.

Recognizing we are each in a different stage of lesbian and gay development, the focus of the coming-out campaign is to encourage every lesbian and gay person in America to take their next step, whatever that may be.

This is a time for political action, action everyone can participate in. In a landmark ruling favoring lesbians and gays (a $3,000,000 anti-gay discrimination class-action suit against Pacific Bell, which with legal fees, etc. was projected to cost Pac Bell $5,000,000), the California Supreme Court, May 31, 1979, said gays and lesbians are protected by California Labor Code which outlaws discrimination based on politics. *The judges interpreted coming out as the most political act, a person can perform.*

SCWU News was on hand at the Gay and Lesbian Pride Parade in June to ask SCWU marchers about their action steps for Coming Out Day.... see pages 5-7

Examples of lesbian/feminist magazines and newsletters in the collections of the Mazer Archives.

"Celebrating the Women in My Life, 1915-200?," a collage on a screen created by Ester Bentley. *Ester Bentley Papers. Photo by Angela Brinskele*

Part II: The Collections of
The June L. Mazer Lesbian Archives

THE HOUR ASSEMBLES ITS ALLIES

BY RED I. AROBATEAU

The Hour Assembles Its Allies. *Red Arobateau Papers*

Making Invisible Histories Visible

Charline Abernathy Papers

COLLECTION ID: 2161
COLLECTION DATES: 1975–1983

A public servant active in Los Angeles, Charline Abernathy was the vice president of the Highland Park Improvement Association, a member and secretary of the Highland Park Chamber of Commerce, and a member of the Board of Directors for North East Youth Foundation. In an effort to be ecologically conscious, she has a mini-farm where she grows her own food. She worked as a building contractor in the Los Angeles area for many years. A welder on aircrafts and ships during World War II, she won an award from Rocketdyne in 1958 for "Most Suggestions." The collection documents her accomplishments and public recognitions and includes articles and plaques recognizing her public service.

ACT UP Papers

COLLECTION ID: 2224
COLLECTION DATES: 1987

Meeting for the first time in West Hollywood in 1987, the Los Angeles chapter of ACT UP (AIDS Coalition to Unleash Power) was inspired by the activities of ACT UP New York. Self defined as a "grass-roots, democratic, militant, direct action organization dedicated to creating positive changes around AIDS in federal and local government, the media and medical industries through nonviolent public protests," the chapter focused on improving access to and quality of AIDS healthcare services, as well as coalition building and other activist communities. Advocating for nonviolent direct action to draw media attention, the group provided training in civil disobedience and conflict resolution and formed support teams to track and respond to confrontations and arrests.

Red Arobateau Papers

COLLECTION ID: 1950
COLLECTION DATES: 1970–1971

Born in 1943, Red Arobateau is a poet, playwright, erotic artist, and painter and a transgender man of mixed-race heritage who identifies as white, Native, Hispanic and African-American. This collection houses several of his self-published poetry collections. Since the poetry collections are self-published, many of the holdings are unique.

Ellen Bass Papers

COLLECTION ID: 2227
COLLECTION DATES: 1987–1990

Ellen Bass is an American poet as well as a co-author of the groundbreaking and still in print book, *The Courage to Heal: A Guide for Women Survivors of Child Sexual Abuse.* She grew up in Margate City, NJ, and attended Goucher College, receiving her bachelor's degree in 1968. She earned her Master's degree from Boston University, studying with Anne

Lesbian News, a news digest founded by Jinx Beers in 1975 and now published by Ella Matthes, is the longest-running lesbian publication in North America. *Jinx Beers Papers.*

Sexton. From 1970 to 1974, Bass worked as an administrator at Project Place, a social service center in Boston. She is currently teaching in the Masters of Fine Arts program at Pacific University in Oregon and has been teaching workshops on "Writing About Our Lives" in Santa Cruz, CA since 1974.

Bass' poems have appeared in hundreds of journals, anthologies and magazines including *Ploughshares, The American Poetry Review* and *The Atlantic Monthly.* Her nonfiction books, including *The Courage to Heal,* have sold over a million copies and have been translated into twelve languages. She has won several awards including a Pushcart Prize, *Missouri Review*'s Larry Levis Award, the Greensboro Poetry Prize and the Elliston Book Award for Poetry.

The collection contains research materials and Betamax® tapes created to accompany *The Courage to Heal,* none of which were ultimately used.

Jinx Beers Papers

COLLECTION ID: 2222
COLLECTION DATES: 1975–2013

Born in Pasadena, CA, in 1933, Jinx Beers was the founder of *Lesbian News* and a lesbian activist. She joined the Air Force, received an honorable discharge, and was active in Reserves for another twelve years until she resigned in 1974 because of policies concerning homosexuals. After earning a B.A. from

UCLA in experimental psychology, she worked at the UCLA Institute for Transportation and Traffic Engineering for eighteen years.

In 1973, Beers co-taught the first lesbian studies class at the Experimental College at UCLA, which served as a connecting point for many Los Angeles activists. Indeed, it yielded a group called "Lesbian Activists." In 1975, she founded *The LN (The Lesbian News)*, a publication of lesbian news that is still published monthly. After fourteen years as the editor and owner, Jinx Beers sold the periodical and began publishing *LSF: Lesbian Short Fiction*. She also managed the business of artist and partner Alicia Austin. In 2008, her memoir, *Memoirs of an Old Dyke*, was published. In 2009, she was honored with a proclamation by the City of West Hollywood as well as with the Etheridge Award for service to the community.

Collection includes personal materials, research and preparatory work for *Memoirs of an Old Dyke*, administrative materials for the magazine *Lesbian News*, stories, and articles.

Ester Bentley Papers

COLLECTION ID: 1981
COLLECTION DATES: 1870–2004

A social worker, lesbian activist and community organizer, Ester Bentley (*shown above*) was born in Louisville, KY, on October 24, 1915. She received her B.S. at Catherine Spalding College in Louisville and completed a Master's in Social Work at the National Catholic School of Social Service at Catholic University of America, Washington, DC. The majority of Bentley's career was spent as a social worker, in both administration and fieldwork. After retiring from her position as a fieldwork consultant at the UCLA School of Social Welfare, she became involved in both Catholic ministries and gay and lesbian organizations. Collection contains personal correspondence, photos, and memorabilia as well as professional research and educational materials.

Mildred Berryman Papers

COLLECTION ID: 2170
COLLECTION DATES: 1918–1990

Mildred Berryman was a researcher, writer, photographer, and stenographer and a lesbian member of the Church of Jesus Christ of Latter-day Saints. She attended Westminster College in Salt Lake City, where she intended to study lesbianism, which the school refused. Berryman married "to try and escape her homosexuality" but soon left her husband. In 1920, Berryman had her first lesbian relationship with a music teacher named Mae Anderson. Their relationship lasted a year. Anderson would eventually become a faculty member of the Latter-day Saint School of Music, teaching alongside Willard Weihe, who was the president of the Bohemian Club, a social group for homosexuals founded in 1886. Around 1920, Berryman joined the LDS Church and received a Patriarchal Blessing in 1921. After another failed attempt at heterosexual marriage, she met Edith Mary Chapman in 1924 and they lived together for four years in Edith's home, which she later turned into a boarding house for lesbians.

Berryman began working as a photographer, processing and taking photographs for the Superior Photo Company. She moved back home and resumed work on her thesis on homosexuality, gathering data for her case studies over the next several years, primarily with people she had met through the Bohemian Club. In her study, she included data on 24 lesbians (including herself) and 9 gay men. In 1936, she met her next companion, known only as Z in case study #24. They were together for twelve years.

In 1939, Berryman stopped working on her thesis, "The Psychological Phenomena of the Homosexual," which she had hoped to turn in to Temple Bar College in Seattle, WA, which may have been an organization operating through correspondence courses. During World War II, Berryman worked at a small arms defense plant at Hill Air Force Base, where she met Ruth Uckerman Dempsey. At the end of the war, the couple opened a manufacturing company called Berryman Novelty Manufacturing. They remained together for thirty-three years until Berryman died at the age of 71. Her obituary lists that she was a member of the Bountiful Community Church, past president of the Business and Professional Women Organization, and past president of the American Legion Auxiliary. Parts of Berryman's unpublished thesis were published in *Signs: Journal of Women in Culture and Society* in 1978. The collection includes research and drafts of her thesis.

Making Invisible Histories Visible

Angela Brinskele Papers

COLLECTION ID: 2158
COLLECTION DATES: 1986–2008

Angela Brinskele has been the Director of Communications of the June L. Mazer Lesbian Archives since 2007. Angela is a professional photographer who has documented the LGBT community since 1984, with a special emphasis on lesbians in Southern California. Brinskele worked for *The Lesbian News* for several years. She has also been a photographer for Outfest for over a decade. Events and organizations that Brinskele has documented include the LA Gay and Lesbian Center, Women On a Roll, Dinah Shore Weekend, and political activist happenings including the "March on the Capitol" that was held in Sacramento in 1991 over AB 101. Collection contains photographs covering gay and lesbian cultural and pride events from 1986 to 2008.

Marion Zimmer Bradley Papers

COLLECTION ID: 1955
COLLECTION DATES: 1959–1999

Born June 3, 1930, in Albany, NY, Marion Zimmer Bradley was interested in science fiction and fantasy as a teenager, participating in amateur fiction contests as an adjunct and as a contestant, most notably for *Fantastic Amazing Stories*

Top: Long Beach Pride Festival, 2012; *above:* Musician at Hamburger Mary's, Newport Beach, 2007 *Photos by Angela Brinskele.*

in 1949. Her first published story, entitled "Women Only" was showcased in *Vortex Science Fiction* in 1953. Always promoting and supporting the work of other writers, Bradley not only encouraged and participated in the world of fan fiction but she also became the editor of anthologies and periodicals supporting up-and-coming authors.

Bradley married Robert Alden Bradley in 1949. They had one child and divorced in 1964. During their marriage, she published her first novel, *The Door Through Space*, which launched her writing career. She also became marginally involved with the lesbian activist organization Daughters of Bilitis. Her novel, *The Planet Savers*, which appeared in 1958, introduced the Darkover world. Her Darkover novels became her most famous book series. Although she wrote the majority of the novels in the series, it was occasionally supplemented by other authors with her blessing and has been continued since her death.

Bradley was active in the gay and lesbian community not just through her writings and bibliographic work but also with counseling services. After becoming ordained in the Eastern Orthodox priesthood (along with her hus-

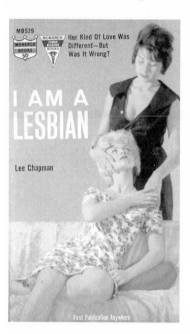

band) by Mikhail Itkin, she volunteered her time at the Gay Pacific Center offering pastoral counseling service. During this time she also published several works under various pseudonyms. Many of these publications were gay and lesbian pulp fiction, most famously the novel *I Am a Lesbian*, which she published in 1962 under the name Lee Chapman.

In 1964, shortly after her divorce from Bradley, Marion married Walter Breen, an American author and numismatist. They collaborated on a bibliography of gay and lesbian literature. They had two children and separated in 1979, but remained married until 1990.

Bradley received her BA from Hardin-Simmons University in Abilene, TX, in 1965. She pursued graduate studies at the University of California, Berkeley until 1967, where she met Diana Paxson, a medieval studies graduate with whom she founded the Society for Creative Anachronism in 1966. During this time in Berkeley, and through the 1970s and 1980s, Bradley considered herself a neo-pagan, developing interests in clairvoyance, extrasensory perception, and reincarnation. She began the Centre for Nontraditional Religion, which hosted various nontraditional groups such as Wiccans. Raised in the Episcopal tradition, she returned to those roots in the 1990s.

In 1979, Marion published what is probably her most famous and groundbreaking work, *The Mists of Avalon*. Working within a feminist, revisionist framework, Bradley retells the Arthurian legend through the lens of its female characters, predominantly through the eyes of Morgaine.

Bradley published her own "The Jewel of Arwen" based on a character in J.R.R. Tolkien's *The Lord of the Rings* Trilogy). In 1984 she began *Sword and Sorceress*, an anthology series devoted to fantasy stories with nontraditional or challenging heroines. She edited the series until her death, and it continued until 2008. In 1988 she began *Marion Zimmer Bradley's Fantasy Magazine*, which published short stories and humorous pieces as well as interviews with recognizable science fiction and fantasy authors. Bradley died on September 25, 1999, after a struggle with heart disease. A year after her death she was awarded with Lifetime Achievement through the World Fantasy Award, which recognizes outstanding achievement in the category of fantasy.

The collection includes two copies of her Gay and Lesbian Bibliography with notations as well as an unpublished manuscript, unedited versions of published materials, brochures from fan gatherings, and some of her husband's work.

Broomstick Magazine Records

COLLECTION ID: 1976
COLLECTION DATES: 1972–2005

An independent, self-published radical feminist magazine dedicated to supporting and promoting women and lesbian activism and art for an audience of women over forty, *Broomstick* was founded in 1978 by Maxine Spencer and Polly Taylor in the San Francisco Bay area. Its main goals focused on confronting ageism, stereotypes of the disabled, and breaking down gender conventions in publishing. Published through 1993, issues explored topics related to radical feminist politics, lesbian culture and art, spirituality of the Crone, women and aging, and feminist coalitions and communities.

As co-editors, Spencer and Taylor intended to develop and expand the mainstream feminist position in support of a growing subculture in the lesbian community that promoted a more radical feminist agenda. *Broomstick* would provide a unique social and political challenge to the feminist literature of its time. The magazine's staff borrowed skills learned from their earlier feminist activities in the late 1960s and early 1970s, such as consciousness raising sessions and feminist networking. *Broomstick*'s editors and contributors hoped that the content would promote a greater understanding of older women's situation. The magazine sought to honor and rescue the image of the Crone—an old woman, often called witch, historically revered as healers and for their wisdom—from public derision. The name *Broomstick* was chosen to symbolize women's shared skills and labor (homemaking), change and improvement (the new broom sweeps clean),

BROOMSTICK

is a unique, reader-participation
magazine by, for, and about
women over forty;
a national communication network
printing the work, experience,
and thoughts
of midlife and older women.

RECENT
BROOMSTICK
TITLES

January is a Drag
Don't Agonize - Organize
Poetry & Politics
Militant Menopausal Woman
A View from the 77th Year
Manifesto of the Older Woman
Over 35 is not Over the Hill
Health Insurance
Pension Plans
The Right to Disagree
Union Maids
On Passing for "Young"
Living in Community
On Changing Names

WE REPOSSESS THE
BROOMSTICK
as a symbol of our strength & unity

It stands for many aspects
of our lives and interests:

SKILLS
homemaking & paid jobs

healing
witches were ancient healers

change
the new broom sweeps clean

POWER
the witch flies on the broom

CONFRONTATION
exposing what society calls ugliness

Promotional brochure for *Broomstick. Broomstick Magazine Records*

BROOMSTICK

STATEMENTS ON LANGUAGE
(Used in drafting editorial comments on manuscripts submitted)

COMMON PHRASES

Perhaps these seem like nit-picking criticisms, but it is just these fami-
liar, customary usages which serve to internalize the sexist/racist attitudes we
learned early in life. We feel that by being perhaps over-careful in eliminat-
ing them, we can remind ourselves and jog the attention of our readers that non-
racist, non-sexist attitudes are important goals for us.

ACCURACY VS POLITICS

Since BROOMSTICK is a political journal, we feel that the content of the
political message is more important than accurately reflecting a protagonist's
thought and speech patterns. So we hope you are willing either to omit ## or to
expand it/comment on it to give recognition to the fact that this reflects a
self-denigration which feminists struggle against.

CANTANKEROUS

We prefer not to use this judgmental term. People who assert their rights
and try to maintain their independence are sometimes labeled "cantankerous" by
those who would prefer them to be docile.

GIRL/LADY

We realize that the people in this story would probably have used "girl"
and "lady" but we are not comfortable with seeing them as the words of the
AUTHOR, which implies your collusion in discounting these women. We call a
human female who is physically mature enough to bear children or earn wages a
WOMAN. She is not a GIRL even if she is 30 years younger than we are. Only a
very young, physically immature human female is a girl.

LADY

To us, "Lady" means an antiseptic, asexual woman who adapts her behavior to
the needs and desires of men. ("Be a Lady" meant, when we were children, "don't
do anything that gets in the way of the men, competes with them, or upsets
them.") "Little Lady" further diminishes us.

"NAG"

"Nag" has become one of those words used to put women (especially wives and
mothers) down. It most often applies to situations where women are given
responsibility for how someone else acts—leaving the husband or child free to
resent the woman instead of taking on responsibility for his own behavior. Can
you find another word here? "Gadfly"?

a bimonthly national magazine by, for, & about women over forty

3543 18th St., san francisco, ca 94110 (415)552-7460

Because of concerns about the perpetuation of stereotypes through language,
many feminist magazines, including *Broomstick*, developed guidelines for editors
and writers. *Broomstick Magazine Records*

WOMEN'S RIGHTS PROJECT

H E L P   W O M E N ' S   S T U D I E S
A N D   B E T T Y   B R O O K S   A T
C A L I F O R N I A   S T A T E   U N I V E R S I T Y
L O N G   B E A C H

ACLU

AMERICAN
CIVIL LIBERTIES UNION
OF SOUTHERN CALIFORNIA
633 S. Shatto Place
Los Angeles, California 90005
Telephone (213) 487-1720

Dear Friends,

The Women's Rights Project of the Southern California Affiliate of the
American Civil Liberties Union is planning to hold a major fundraiser this
September 10th at Fritchman Auditorium from 6:30 to midnight in an effort
to support current initiatives of the Project. Tentative plans call for a
gala evening of food, drink, and lively entertainment.

This year a major issue of concern for the Women's Rights Project has been
the pernicious attack upon feminism and academic freedom by supporters of
the New Right. Proceeds from the fundraiser will go for the support of
ACLU litigation on behalf of the defense of the Women's Studies Program at
Cal State Long Beach, which has been singled out for attack by these
forces of repression.

I would personally like to invite your participation in the planning of
this fundraiser on Thursday, July 7 at American Broadcasting Company, 4151
Prospect, Hollywood, California 90027. For more information call June
Briggs at 557-5353. At that time, subcommittees will be chosen for
program development, publicity and refreshments.

In planning for an event of this size we desperately need the assistance
of many volunteers, especially from those who stand committed to the
struggle for women's rights and academic freedom. Please join us on July
7 to lend your skills and talents to the planning of this important event.

For further information please call: Trish Kelliher at (213) 988-5800 or
(213) 873-4434 or Rose Ash at (714) 620-2189 or (714) 626-7816. Thank you
for your support. We look forward to working with you.

Sincerely,

Trish Kelliher

Trish Kelliher, Chairperson
ACLU Women's Rights
Fundraising Project

PLEASE POST
June 2, 1983
SM/LH

Appeal letter from the ACLU for the lawsuit over the Women's
Studies Program at California State University, Long Beach.
California State University, Long Beach Records

power (the witch flies on the broom), healing (the witch as
ancient healer), and speaking out about what society consid-
ers ugly. Collection includes a complete run of the magazine,
organizational records, financial statements, correspondence,
submissions and rejections, and many of the plates used for
printing the magazine. Collection also contains some of
Spencer's personal papers.

California State University,
Long Beach Records

COLLECTION ID: 2201
COLLECTION DATES: 1974–1991

The first Women's Studies courses were taught at California
State University, Long Beach (CSULB) in the early 1970s. In
1974, the Center for Women's Studies was formed by faculty
and students with the goal of developing an interdisciplinary minor within American Studies and to open a women's
resource center. Around this same time, the Associated Students opened a student-run Women's Referral Center in the
Student Union. The content of some courses was controversial. There were also on-campus debates regarding whether
the referral center should become a women's resource center.
In 1982, activists targeted the center. As a result, program
director Sondra Hale and Women's Center director Denise
Wheeler were fired. In response, thirteen faculty member

and three students filed a lawsuit with the ACLU against
the university, charging violations of the First and Fourth
Amendments. This collection contains files pertaining to the
lawsuit, including financial records, memos, memoranda, correspondence, newspaper clippings, community reports, and
other community organizing documentation.

Betsy Calloway Papers

COLLECTION ID: 2164
COLLECTION DATES: 1971–1976

In the 1970s, Betsy Calloway owned and operated a feminist
publishing, graphic design, and printing business. Maud
Gonne Press was named after the Irish revolutionary, feminist, and actress. Collection contains some personal correspondence from Calloway, but the majority of the material
focuses on her business. Examples of the press' work, correspondence between clients, and catalogs of comparable businesses serving the lesbian feminist community are contained.

Marie Cartier Papers

COLLECTION ID: 1953
COLLECTION DATES: 1988–2010

Currently teaching in the
film department at UC
Irvine and in the Wom-
en's Studies department at
California State University,
Northridge, Marie Cartier
is a teacher, poet, writer,
healer, artist, activist and
facilitator, as well as the
holder of a first-degree
blackbelt in karate.

Her poetry is widely
published. Many of her
poems have been included
in publications such as
Sinister Wisdom, *Heresies*,
Colorado State Review,
Culture Concrete, and
Central Park, as well

Marie Cartier (*right*) with friend,
Long Beach Pride Festival, 2009.
Photo by Angela Brinskele

as being included in several poetry anthologies, including
Wanting Women and *Poetry of Sex*. She has written five plays,
all originally published by Dialogus Press. *Stumbling into
Light* incorporates monologue, poetry and Greek chorus
to explore a woman's healing path from sexual trauma and
abuse. *Leave a Light on When You Go Out* utilizes both drama
and humor through the style of performance poetry to
deal with issues of violence against women. *Freeze Count* is
adapted from original oral histories conducted with inmates
at the Wyoming Women's Center. *Close to Home* is a more
traditional play, humorously exploring the attempt for a
mother and daughter to find common ground.

Collection contains her academic work from Claremont
Graduate University; published and unpublished creative

LESBIAN WRITERS SERIES 1989

JANUARY 21

JOAN NESTLE
CO-SPONSORED BY UCLA'S
WOMEN STUDIES DEPARTMENT & THE
CENTER FOR THE STUDY OF WOMEN

FEBRUARY 18

SUSIE BRIGHT

MARCH 18

KITTY TSUI   WILLYCE KIM

APRIL 15

DOROTHY ALLISON   ROBIN PODOLSKY

MAY 20

MICHELLE CLIFF   AYOFEMIE STOWE

JUNE 17

CAROLYN WEATHERS   GEORGIA COTRELL

JULY 15

ALEIDA RODRIGUEZ   JESSIE LATTIMORE

AUGUST 19

TERRY WOLVERTON   BIA LOWE

SEPTEMBER 16

CHERRIE MORAGA   ANA CASTILLO

OCTOBER 21

KATHERINE FORREST

NOVEMBER 18

ELOISE KLEIN HEALY   SHARON STRICKER

DECEMBER 16

MARIE-CLAIRE BLAIS
CO-SPONSORED BY THE LOS ANGELES
QUEBEC GOVERNMENT OFFICE

ORGANIZER

ANN BRADLEY

A DIFFERENT LIGHT BOOKSTORE
4014 SANTA MONICA BLVD.
LOS ANGELES, CA   90029
(213) 668-0629

ALL READINGS ARE ON THE
THIRD SATURDAY OF THE
MONTH AT 8 P.M.

Sophia Corleone and Gail Suber organized the Lesbian Writers Series of readings. *Kitty Tsui Papers*

Making Invisible Histories Visible

writing projects including plays, short stories, poetry and fiction; flyers from performances for local artists as well as for herself; ephemera from performances; documents relating to the Dandelion Warriors incest survivors work; and personal papers relating to job searches, grants, and project proposals. Also included is a large collection of published books and a selection of periodicals and organizational publications and calendars.

Jane Clewe Papers

COLLECTION ID: 2190
COLLECTION DATES: 1970–2009

A graduate of Princeton University in 1977, Jane Clewe was an active member of the Wilderness Women and a donor to and member of many activist and community organizations devoted to lesbian and women's issues. She lived with her partner Debbie in Los Angeles and enjoyed hiking, scuba and other outdoors activities. Collection contains materials collected and maintained by Clewe, including a substantial number of magazines from the 1990s focused on women's and lesbian issues as well as newsletters and communication from a number of activist and community organizations devoted to lesbian and gay issues in Los Angeles.

Nikki Colodny Papers

COLLECTION ID: 2188
COLLECTION DATES: 1978–1995

Dr. Nikki Colodny was an abortion provider, women's health advocate, and activist operating in Toronto, Ontario, Canada, throughout the 1980s and 1990s. Most prominently, she worked with Dr. Henry Morgentaler, providing medical care and abortion services, which at the time were illegal. Their arrests and repeated harassment brought publicity to their cause, eventually precipitating the 1988 overturn of the abortion law by the Supreme Court of Canada.

In 1988, Colodny founded the cooperative Women's Choice Health Clinic. In addition to her medical services, she was an active participant in several pro-choice organizations, including the Ontario Coalition of Abortion Clinics (OCAC), the National Abortion Federation (NAF), and the Canadian Abortion Rights Action League (CARAL). Her research is widely published in both medical and women's studies academic journals.

Collection contains some organizational records from the Choice in Health Clinic as well as from several operational Canadian pro-choice activist organizations. Also included is press coverage of abortion rights in Canada as well as more specific coverage of Dr. Nikki Colodny and Dr. Henry Morgentaler. Research materials and a small number of photographs and personal correspondence are present in the collection.

Sophia Corleone Papers

COLLECTION ID: 1988
COLLECTION DATES: 1973–1994

Sophia Corleone (along with co-coordinator Gail Suber) organized the Lesbian Writers Series of readings at A Different Light Bookstore in the Silver Lake neighborhood of Los Angeles, CA. A graduate of Smith College, Corleone wrote fiction, memoirs, and essays. Collection contains materials relevant to the planning of the series, as well as her own personal research materials, flyers, and newsletters related to community organizations and events.

Renee Cote Papers

COLLECTION ID: 2197
COLLECTION DATES: 1984–1987

Renee Cote was a psychotherapist and lesbian activist. Collection includes her thesis, "From 49 to -9: The Beginnings of my Recovery as an ACMIP (Adult Child of Mentally Ill Parent)," submitted in March of 1987 to Vermont College of Norwich University. Also included is a copy of *La Journee internationale des femmes* by Renee Cote, which was published in 1984.

Daughters of Bilitis Records

COLLECTION ID: 1946
COLLECTION DATES: 1955–1986

The Daughters of Bilitis was founded by four lesbian couples in San Francisco in 1955. Its original purpose was to counteract the loneliness they felt as lesbians, though the organization increasingly began to focus on educating lesbians about their rights and on lobbying. The organization began publishing a newsletter, *The Ladder*, in 1956, and had expanded to five chapters across the U.S. by 1959.

National conventions were held starting in 1960 and included members and speakers from across the country. The conventions provided members the opportunity to discuss the organization, and the group's original focus on conformity and integration soon became a heated topic. Many members wanted to see the organization more involved in the direct action politics that were increasingly employed by other organizations as the 1960s progressed. Conflict within the organization, between the San Francisco and New York chapters in particular, continued, and the National Chapter eventually disbanded in 1970. Local chapters continued to function independently, although *The Ladder* ceased publication in 1972.

Collection includes documents related to the organization's national and local chapters. The collection also includes personal correspondence between two of its original founders, Phyllis Lyon and Del Martin, and documents from several other homophile organizations.

Program for
Third National
Convention,
1964. *Daugh-
ters of Bilitis
Records*

THE THRESHOLD
of the
FUTURE

PROGRAM

Friday,
June 19:   COCKTAIL PARTY AND RECEPTION

8:30 p.m.   New York Chapter Office, 441 West 28th Street,
            New York City. Speakers, guests, members and
            friends are invited.

Saturday,
June 20:   PUBLIC FORUM

            The Barbizon Room of the Barbizon-Plaza Hotel,
            106 Central Park South, New York City.

9:00 a.m.   Registration. Forum sessions are open to the
            public.

9:30   ADDRESS OF WELCOME
            Cleo Glenn, National President of Daughters of
            Bilitis, Inc.

10:00   HOMOSEXUALITY, THE PRESENT AND THE FUTURE
            Wardell B. Pomeroy, Ph.D., co-author of Sexual
            Behavior in the Human Female and Sexual Behav-
            ior in the Human Male.

10:50   THE SOCIAL SITUATION OF THE HOMOSEXUAL
            Ernest van den Haag, Ph.D., author of The Fab-
            ric of Society and Education as an Industry.

11:40   SOCIOLOGICAL RESEARCH TABOOS, PAST AND PRESENT
            Sylvia Fava, Ph.D., co-editor of Sexual Behav-
            ior in American Society: An Appraisal of the
            First Two Kinsey Reports.

12:30 p.m.   MORE LESBIANS THAN
                NON-LESBIANS REPORT RAPE - WHY?
            Ralph H. Gundlach, Ph.D., Associate Director
            of Research at the Postgraduate Center for
            Mental Health. (This preliminary report is
            the result of research being conducted with
            the cooperation of Daughters of Bilitis, Inc.)

1:20   LUNCHEON IN THE NORTH GALLERY
            Speaker: Rev. Robert W. Wood, Pastor of the
            First Congregational Church of Spring Valley,
            New York; author of Christ and the Homosexual.
                Topic: LYDIA AND DEBORAH

2:45   WHITHER THE HOMOPHILE MOVEMENT?
            Donald Webster Cory, considered by many "the
            father of the homophile movement"; author of
            The Homosexual in America and the forthcoming
            The Lesbian in America.

3:30   THE ESSENCE OF FEMININITY
                A Panel Discussion

            Moderator: Jess Stearn, author of The Sixth
                        Man and The Grapevine.

            Panelists: Mrs. Lee Steiner, marriage coun-
                        selor, author and eminent radio
                        personality.

                        Adele Kenyon, author of Fourteen
                        Days to a New Figure and How To
                        Exercise Without Really Trying.

                        Florence DeSantis, Fashion Editor
                        for Bell Syndicate.

4:50   SEXUAL FREEDOM AND HOPE FOR THE FUTURE
            Robert Veit Sherwin, New York attorney; author
            of Sex and the Statutory Law.

5:40   IS CHANGE NECESSARY? or HOW TO ENJOY LIVING!
            Mildred Weiss, Ph.D., former Captain of the
            Intelligence Corps of the U. S. Air Force;
            formerly Chief Psychologist of the Cleveland
            (Ohio) Center on Alcoholism; now Assistant
            Professor and Administrative Officer of the
            Psychology Dept., Western Reserve University.

6:30   HOMOSEXUALITY AND THE CURRENT SCENE
            Gerald Sabath, Ph.D., practicing psychoanalyst
            and lecturer associated with the Postgraduate
            Center for Mental Health.

7:20   COCKTAIL HOUR IN THE LOWER LOUNGE

8:30   BANQUET IN THE NORTH GALLERY
            Speaker: Rev. C. Edward Egan, Jr., pastor of
            a Methodist church on Long Island; well-known
            counselor of "persons who by reason of their
            sexual deviation are in trouble with them-
            selves, the law, or society."
                Topic: WOMEN'S WORLD OF TOMORROW

Sunday,
June 21:   GENERAL ASSEMBLY OF DAUGHTERS OF BILITIS, INC.

9:00 a.m.   New York Chapter Office, 441 West 28th Street,
            New York City. Business meeting for members
            of the organization only.

Monday,
June 22:   CLOSE OF GENERAL ASSEMBLY. SIGHTSEEING TOUR.

10:00 a.m. New York Chapter Office. Completion of unfin-
            ished General Assembly business.

            Sightseeing tour of "The Big City." Non-mem-
            bers are welcome.

DAUGHTERS OF BILITIS, INC. wishes to take this opportunity
to extend its gratitude to everyone who has helped in the
presentation of this convention.

DAUGHTERS
OF
BILITIS

Third
National

CONVENTION

New York City
June 19-22, 1964

Elizabeth Gould Davis Papers

COLLECTION ID: 2169
COLLECTION DATES: 1990–1999

Elizabeth Gould Davis was an American lesbian librarian and author. Born in Kansas in 1910, she earned her Master's degree in librarianship at the University of Kentucky in 1951 and worked as a librarian in Sarasota, FL. In 1971, she wrote and published the feminist text *The First Sex*. In *The First Sex*, she made many controversial and provocative arguments, asserting that congenital killers and criminals have two Y chromosomes and that society has been diverted from its natural state of being governed by matriarchies. She passed away in 1974. Collection consists of an unpublished manuscript, *The Female Principle*, which was the planned follow-up to *The First Sex*.

Pat Denslow Papers

COLLECTION ID: 2163
COLLECTION DATES: 1981–1984

Pat Denslow was a lesbian activist and organizer. She worked with both the Southern California Women for Understanding (SCWU) as well as Old Lesbians Organizing for Change (OLOC). She graduated from UCLA and briefly worked with Pacifica Radio. Collection includes interviews, drafts, and the final product of the Elderbond project.

Business card of Diana Press. *Diana Press Records*

Diana Press Records

COLLECTION ID: 2135
COLLECTION DATES: 1970–1994

Diana Press was a women's print shop and feminist publishing house began by Coletta Reid and Katherine "Casey" Czarnik in Baltimore, Maryland in 1972. Originally an instant print shop, their first publishing effort was the publication in 1972 of Rita Mae Brown's second poetry collection *Songs to a Handsome Woman*, which became a bestseller for the press. They also published the second edition of *The Hand that Cradles the Rock*. Over the next three years Diana Press grew into a full-service publishing house, releasing an assortment

of feminist books and calendars, most notably works by Brown and poet Judy Grahn; *The Lesbians Home Journal*, an anthology of stories from the celebrated lesbian magazine *The Ladder*; and a reprint of Dr. Jeannette Foster's pioneering book, *Sex Variant Women in Literature*.

On October 25, 1977, Diana Press was hit by a crippling act of vandalism which destroyed thousands of copies of books and damaged essential printing equipment. Losses were estimated to total as much as $100,000. The feminist community responded with letters of support, donations, and benefits, but the Press was unable to sustain the financial impact of the incident. Works by the likes of Judy Chicago, Kathy Zozachenko, Elizabeth Gould Davis, Pat Parker, and Judy Grahn, which had been scheduled for publication, were never released. Plagued by financial troubles, the vandalism, and disagreements within the leadership, Diana ceased publishing in 1979.

Despite the misfortune and controversy, Diana Press is a notable example of a feminist alternative and challenge to the established publishing world. Collection contains a rich assortment of administrative materials; author and project files; manuscripts and poetry; press and distribution materials; and correspondence. Items date from 1970 to 1994, with the bulk dating from 1972 to 1979.

Sylvia Dobson Papers

COLLECTION ID: 1989
COLLECTION DATES: 1934–1992

Born in 1908, Sylvia Dobson was a schoolteacher, an aspiring writer, and a well-known correspondent and friend of the modernist and imagist poet H.D. (Hilda Doolittle). They had a brief courtship, then were friends for nearly thirty years. Collection contains their correspondence and some research materials.

Sandy Dwyer Papers

COLLECTION ID: 2166
COLLECTION DATES: 1977–1991

Born Sandra Jean Nelson in Milwaukee, WI, Sandy Dwyer is a lesbian activist, playwright, and journalist living and working in Los Angeles, CA. She received a Master's at the University of Missouri and spent time as a trapeze artist, biology teacher, trick-rope artist, social worker, gardener, actor and playwright. Coming out as a lesbian in 1986, she became involved with the gay and lesbian community in Los Angeles. She co-founded *The News*, which focused on local gay and lesbian news and events and was known for its hard-hitting journalism and gained notoriety for exposing financial abuses by large mainstream gay and lesbian nonprofit organizations.

Collection contains materials used and produced by Dwyer predominantly in the 1970s and 1980s. Included are plays written by Dwyer as well as programs and other promotional materials from theater productions in which she was involved. Personal and professional correspondence are also included.

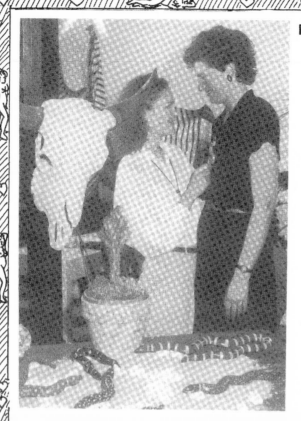
Inspired by Donna Deitch's *Desert Hearts* (1985), Linda Farin produced and marketed *Waking Up:
A Lesson in Love,* a lesbian erotic video. *Linda Farin Papers*

Marsha Epstein Papers

COLLECTION ID: 2220
COLLECTION DATES: 1960–2013

In 1974 and 1975, Martha Epstein worked for the women's clinic at the Gay and Lesbian Services Center in Los Angeles. From 1975 to 1979, she was the Medical Director of Herself Health Clinic, a women's clinic run by a cooperative of radical lesbians for the women in the community. Epstein attended medical school at UC San Francisco; and received a Master's of Public Medicine, Health in Epidemiology from UC Berkeley. After completing a Fellowship in Family Planning at UCLA, she started working in family planning, performing abortions for Los Angeles County briefly.

Epstein had a private medical practice for four years. After the birth of her son, she worked for the Los Angeles County Public Health System for twenty-eight years, serving as a District Health Officer for thirteen years, Area Medical Director for twelve years, and transferred to Chronic Disease Prevention. She developed a tobacco cessation continuing education program online and educated primary care doctors about tobacco cessation.

An LGBT activist who was an advocate for the inclusion of bisexual accounts in the history of the gay rights movement, Epstein is a subject in the documentary *On These Shoulders We Stand*, an account of early gay life and activism in Los Angeles. She is also an active volunteer and participant in the Los Angeles Jewish community, through her work with the synagogue Beth Chayim Chadashim.

Linda Farin Papers

COLLECTION ID: 1942
COLLECTION DATES: 1986–1989

A successful lawyer in Austin, TX, Linda Farin became inspired to produce a realistic and positive lesbian erotic film after seeing Donna Deitch's *Desert Hearts*. Through her participation with Liatris Media, which produced the Third Wave Women's International Film and Video Festival from 1986 to 1989, Farin met Greta Schiller and Andrea Weiss. Schiller became involved in the project in the early stages anonymously but later added her name to the project as director. Collection documents the production, distribution, and reception of the film *Waking Up: A Lesson in Love*, which was produced and co-written by Farin, including drafts, financial documents, advertising strategies, copy reviews, correspondence, and VHS copies of the film, interviews, and auditions.

Martha Foster Papers

COLLECTION ID: 1990
COLLECTION DATES: 1925–1986

Martha Foster was a poet and fiction writer who lived in Los Angeles, CA. This collection includes correspondence, photographs, and manuscripts.

Top and bottom: Martha Foster. Martha Foster Papers

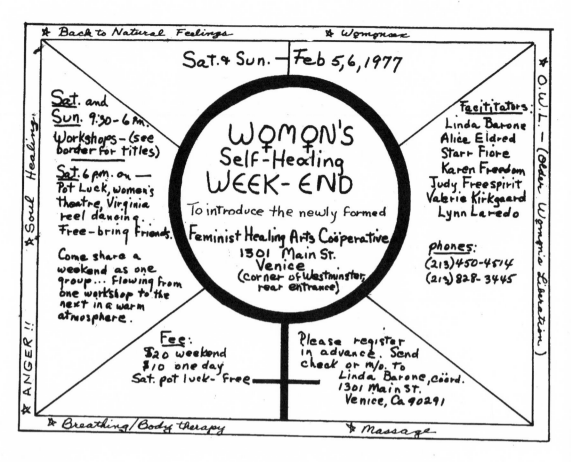

Sat. & Sun. — Feb 5, 6, 1977

* Back to Natural Feelings   * Womonsex

* O.W.L. — (Older Womonia Liberation)

* Soul Healing

WOMON'S Self-Healing WEEK-END
To introduce the newly Formed
Feminist Healing Arts Coöperative.
1301 Main St.
Venice
(corner of Westminster,
rear entrance)

Sat. and Sun. 9:30-6 P.M. Workshops – (see border for titles)

Sat. 6 P.M. on — Pot Luck, women's theatre, Virginia reel dancing. Free – bring friends.

Come share a weekend as one group... Flowing from one workshop to the next in a warm atmosphere.

Facilitators:
Linda Barone
Alice Eldred
Starr Fiore
Karen Freedom
Judy Freespirit
Valerie Kirkgaard
Lynn Laredo

phones:
(213)450-4514
(213)828-3445

* ANGER!!

Fee:
$20 weekend
$10 one day
Sat. pot luck - free

Please register in advance. Send check or m/o. to Linda Barone, coörd. 1301 Main St. Venice, Ca 90291

* Breathing/Body therapy   * Massage

Judy Freespirit Papers

COLLECTION ID: 1956
COLLECTION DATES: 1971–1983

Judy Freespirit was born Judith Louise Berkowitz in 1936 in inner-city Detroit, Michigan to a working-class Jewish family of East-ern European descent. She often pointed to her early life as formative for her political and activist work later, as well as crediting theatre and dancing as positive outlets for frustration. An incest survivor who was pressured to diet beginning at age eight, Freespirit developed a love of the stage and a well-defined sense of humor. She was a life-long activist and advocate for Jewish, lesbian and fat rights.

Freespirit attended Michigan State University for two years and majored in drama before marrying. She, her son, and her husband moved to Los Angeles in 1960 where she finished college and began her work in the psychiatric field, finishing her Master's degree at the age of 35. Through her discovery of the Women's Liberation Movement and her professional background, Judy developed and began to share her Radical Therapy skills with the feminist community. During this period, she also came out as a lesbian and left her husband. Along with four others, she founded the Fat Underground in 1976. After moving to the Bay Area, she founded the Fat Lip Reader's Theatre, a collective of fat women writers and performers. In 1978, Freespirit became involved in working to stop the Briggs Initiative and traveled around California raising awareness and funds for its defeat. After its defeat, she moved to the Berkeley/Oakland area

and became more focused on her Jewish identity, involving herself in a Jewish Lesbian Writer's group.

Suffering with asthma and severe allergies, Judy became active in the disability movement, working with the World Institute on Disabilities. Throughout the 1980s and 90s, Freespirit wrote and performed prolifically, creating one woman shows dealing with her life as a fat, Jewish, lesbian incest survivor with disabilities. She published in journals, spoke at health conferences, provided counseling, and made people laugh. Up until her death in 2008, she remained an advocate, calling for more visibility of the gay and lesbian community in elder care housing.

This collection includes materials with her married name, Judith Ackerman, because she continued to use it for legal purposes. It also contains written and published materials, as well as other materials that are part of her personal collection of political writings and community information. The bulk of the writings in this collection are focused on her fat activism, specifically through her involvement with both Radical Ther-apy practices and the Fat Underground.

Linda Garber

COLLECTION ID: 1958
COLLECTION DATES: 1990–1994

Linda Garber is an associate professor of Women's and Gen-der Studies at Santa Clara University. In 1987, she received her B.A. from Harvard in English and American Literature. She also received her teaching credentials in the same year

FAT WOMEN WANTED

TO ORGANIZE NATIONAL CONFERENCE

```
**********************************************************
*  MEETING IS OPEN TO FAT WOMEN WHO SUPPORT THE BASIC CONCEPTS  *
*  OF FAT LIBERATION. (NAMELY: THIS IS NOT A PRO-WEIGHT LOSS/   *
*  MAINTENANCE CONFERENCE.)    FOR FURTHER INFORMATION CALL:    *
*         826-1444 (S.F.) or 652-4843 (E.Bay)                   *
**********************************************************
```

FIRST MEETING:
SUN., SEPT. 18, 1983,   7–10 PM
50 FELL st., S.F.
(NEW COLLEGE LAW SCHOOL ~ BTW. MKT. & VAN NESS)

```
**********************************************************
*  WHEELCHAIR ACCESSIBLE;        A.S.L.;        CHILDCARE.  *
*                                                           *
*  Please refrain from wearing perfumes or scented cosmetics in *
*       consideration of women with environmental ilness.   *
**********************************************************
```

mk/labor donated

Flyer for meeting to organize national conference in support of
Fat Liberation. *Judy Freespirit Papers*

**Anti–Rape
Conference**
Saturday, June 16
Noon–5PM

Flyer for Anti-Rape Conference. *Judy Freespirit Papers*

March with onlookers. *Diane Germain Papers*

Diane Germain, Califia commnity, 1982. *Diane Germain Papers*

from Harvard. She received her M.A. from Stanford University in the Modern Thoughts and Literature program in 1990 and completed her Ph.D. in the same department in 1995. She has held positions at both Santa Clara University and California State University Fresno.

She has authored *Identity Poetics: Race, Class, and the Lesbian-Feminist Roots of Queer Theory* (New York: Columbia University Press, 2001) and *Tilting the Tower: Lesbians/ Teaching/Queer Subjects* (New York: Routledge, 1994), and edited *Lesbian Sources: A Bibliography of Periodical Articles, 1 9 7 0 – 1 9 9 0* (New York: Garland, 1993). While the collection has a few items relating to the *Lesbian Studies Reader* and other academic activities, the majority of the collection covers the publication of the anthology, *Tilting the Tower*, including collecting, editing, permissions, and revisions.

Gay and Lesbian Community Services Center Records

COLLECTION ID: 2204
COLLECTION DATES: 1975–1992

The Los Angeles Gay and Lesbian Center is a clinic serving lesbian, gay, bisexual and transgender people in Los Angeles. Its former name was the Gay and Lesbian Community Services Center. The collection contains institutional documents as well as programming and event information. This collection includes promotional materials, correspondence and organizational documents regarding the programming, campaigns and activities of the Los Angeles Gay and Lesbian Center from 1975 to 1991.

Diane Germain Papers

COLLECTION ID: 1961
COLLECTION DATES: 1956–2010

Diane Germain is a French-American lesbian-feminist psychiatric social worker. She conducts the Lesbian History Project and created and conducted a strength group for Women Survivors of Incest and/or childhood molestation for five years. She was one of the founding members of Dykes on Hikes, The Lesbian Referral Services, Beautiful Lesbian Thespians and California Women's Art Collective. She was an early principal member of the San Diego Lesbian Organization and a collective member of both Las Hermanas and the Califia community. She worked at Lambda Archives throughout the 1990s, interviewing women in order to preserve lesbian history and gathering collections. She later returned to serve as the Student Volunteer Coordinator.

She was the staff cartoonist for *HotWire: The Journal of Women's Music, Culture of Chicago* and *Lesbian News*. She is featured in both the anthology *Tomboys!*, edited by Lynne Yamaguchi and Karen Barber, and *Lesbian Culture: An Anthology*. Germain was not only interested in documenting her own experiences but also in documenting the representation of women in the media and preserving lesbian culture on the whole for posterity. Therefore, the content of this collection is varied. The collection contains materials from activist organizations in which Germain was herself involved, as well as information and resources for other like-minded organizations. She also collected magazine and newspaper clippings that included her art work. The collection also includes financial documents and other organizational records relating

Diane Germain, early 1950s. *Diane Germain Papers*

A chance to make HISTORY

Jackie Goldberg
City Council

On June 8 we can make history by electing *Jackie Goldberg* as the first openly lesbian member of the Los Angeles City Council!

Jackie has always been an uncompromising, passionate fighter for our issues.

Don't let the opportunity pass! Join us now!

You can volunteer or make donations to Jackie's campaign by calling

(213) 665-5576

Flyer for Jackie Goldberg's campaign for Los Angeles City Council. She was elected and became the first openly lesbian member. *Jackie Goldberg Papers*

to the coffee house Las Hermanas, and presentations meant to be given the Califia community. Materials also include videotapes of community events and speakers and a significant amount of ephemera and realia.

Gertrude's Café Records

COLLECTION ID: 2137
COLLECTION DATES: 1975–1979

In the fall of 1975, a group of women opened Gertrude's Silver Eighth Note Café in Eugene, OR, with the idea of supporting a women's center. The restaurant functioned as a collective and food was priced inexpensively. Gertrude's Café often offered activities in the visual and performing arts, including music performances, poetry readings, and displays of painting and photography. In 1976, a radical left group was invited to buy the building where Gertrude's rented space, but the two groups never reached a lease agreement and the café was evicted. About a year later, a group containing original supporters and new supporters opened a second restaurant at 12th and Lincoln, but it did not survive. Collection contains documents related to its general history, operation, finances, and eventual dissolution.

Jackie Goldberg Papers

COLLECTION ID: 2196
COLLECTION DATES: 1993

An openly lesbian politician, teacher, and member of the Democratic Party, Jackie Goldberg is a former member of the California State Assembly. A graduate of Morningside High School in Inglewood, CA, Goldberg graduated from the UC Berkeley, where she was a member of SLATE, the leftist student organization, and a major player in the Free Speech Movement while on campus. She also holds a Master's degree in education from the University of Chicago.

Goldberg was a teacher in Compton Unified School District, she served on and was later president of the Board of Education of the Los Angeles Unified School District and a member of the Los Angeles City Council. She was elected to represent the 45th district in the California State Assembly in November 2000 and was re-elected in 2002 and 2004. She was a founding member of the California Legislative LGBT Caucus and a founding member of the Progressive Caucus in Sacramento. Collection represents materials the campaign of Jackie Goldberg for City Council in Los Angeles in 1993. Included are campaign materials and news coverage.

Degania Golove Papers

COLLECTION ID: 1984
COLLECTION DATES: 1981–1999

Degania Golove is an activist and historian primarily focusing on lesbian history. A longtime volunteer and one-time coordinator of the Mazer Archives, she is consistently acknowledged for her research assistance with gay and lesbian

One of the many periodicals that Barbara Grier collected between 1972 and 1992. *Barbara Grier Periodical Collection*

historical work. She has received the Women in Leadership Award from the West Hollywood Chamber of Commerce in acknowledgment of her community and activist work.

This collection contains research that Golove compiled for a survey of women's studies, lesbian studies, and feminist studies syllabi in college and university curriculum. The collection includes correspondence between Golove and various researchers, professors, and educators, and course syllabi and brief biographies of contributors.

Barbara Grier Periodical Collection

COLLECTION ID: 2130
COLLECTION DATES: 1972–1992

A well-known writer, publisher, and lesbian-feminist activist, Barbara Grier was born in Cincinnati, OH, and spent most of her life in the Midwest. An anomaly for her time, Grier came out early, in 1945 at the age of twelve, reportedly announcing the fact to her mother after researching homosexuality at her local library. At sixteen she began collecting lesbian-themed books, which she dubbed "Lesbiana," a passion she maintained throughout her life. In 1967 Grier, along with Lee Stuart, published *The Lesbian in Literature*, an attempt to compile a bibliography of all known lesbian-themed books as well as books with lesbian characters. Two subsequent editions were published in 1975 and 1981.

In her early years, Grier wrote for several homophile publications including *ONE* and *Mattachine Review*; however, she is most remembered for her work with *The Ladder*, the monthly magazine published by the Daughters of Bilitis, the first national lesbian organization in the United States. Writing under the pseudonyms Gene Damon, Vern Niven, and Lennox Strong, Grier began contributing copy to *The Ladder* in 1957, and continued until 1968 when she assumed the role of editor, and then publisher, in 1970. Under her guidance, the magazine grew in size and readership, espousing increasingly radical feminist ideals, until its contentious dissolution in 1972.

In 1973, Grier co-founded Naiad Books, which later became Naiad Press, the preeminent lesbian book publisher that advanced the careers of writers such as Katherine Forrest, Sarah Schulman, Lee Lynch, Isabelle Miller, Barbara Wilson, and Valerie Taylor. Conceived of as a movement press, Naiad is credited with opening up lesbian writing to the world, publishing over five hundred books of romance, history, poetry, erotica, and science fiction, as well as reprinting canonical out-of-print lesbian works by authors such as Jane Rule, Ann Bannon, Gale Wilhelm, and Gertrude Stein. Naiad's controversial 1985 nonfiction publication *Lesbian Nuns: Breaking Silence* was banned in Boston and resulted in numerous talk-show appearances for Grier. Bella Books purchased Naiad's list when Grier and her partner Donna McBride retired in 2003.

Pembroke Park, by Michelle Martin, was published by Naiad Press. *Woman's Building Records*

Compiled and donated by Grier, the collection represents a rich assemblage of feminist and lesbian newspapers, magazines, journals, and small press publications. Although this collection spans the years 1969 to 1992, the bulk is from the 1980s and features periodicals from large U.S. metropolitan areas as well as smaller towns. Several titles come from Canada, and one from England. A notable strength of the collection is the range in type of periodical—ad heavy weekly LGBT newspapers such as Pittsburgh's *Out*, newsletters from such organizations as Seattle's Lesbian Resource Center, bibliographic resources including the University of Wisconsin's Feminist Periodicals, and personal publications such as Dorothy Feola's Women's Network. The collection also contains a small amount of other materials: Grier's

correspondence, dealing primarily with reviews of Naiad books and advertising; press clippings and materials relating to *Lesbian Nuns*; and a 1985 audio recording with Grier.

Gianna Groves-Lord Papers

COLLECTION ID: 2138
COLLECTION DATES: 1950–1993

Gianna Groves-Lord was a professional chef who later turned to floristry. She was as a caterer in England in 1960 and came to the U.S. through employment with the South African Embassy. She found herself as the only "lady chef" on Embassy Row in Washington, DC. Hired by Harriet Deutsch, she moved to California. She later gave up catering and began work with Pierre Kenards Custom Florist in 1975. Collection largely consists of personal records related to immigration and employment. Also included are financial documents, correspondence, materials on hobbies and health, newspaper clippings, and photographs.

Barbara Guest Papers

COLLECTION ID: 1992
COLLECTION DATES: 1980–1985

Barbara Guest was an American poet and prose stylist who gained prominence in the 1950s and 1960s as an active member of the New York School. The collection includes a manuscript titled "Herself Defined: A Biography of the Poet H.D." Poet/writer H.D. (Hilda Doolittle) was an outspoken bisexual.

Roma Guy Papers

COLLECTION ID: 2160
COLLECTION DATES: 1965–1977

An activist who worked for health education, an end to homelessness, and for lesbian feminist politics, Roma Guy was born in Maine and received her undergraduate degree in both sociology and history from the University of Maine and a Master's in Social Work from Wayne State University. Since the early 1970s, she and her partner, Diana Jones, have lived and worked in San Francisco.

Guy was a founder of the San Francisco Women's Building and the Stay in School Family Resource Center at San Francisco State University and was the executive director of The Women's Foundation. Throughout the 1990s, she served on the Board of Directors of the Oakland-based Institute for Social and Economic Studies, which fostered alliances among progressives and leftists. As of 2005, Guy was a lecturer in the San Francisco State University's Department of Health Education and served on the San Francisco City and county Health Commission in addition to serving as the director of the Bay Area Homelessness Program. This collection contains writings and materials collected during her work and activist activities.

Lesbian Connection

March/April 1993

Vol. 15, Iss. 5

Free to Lesbians, but the suggested donation is $3/issue, more if you can, less if you can't

---

March/April 1933 issue of *Lesbian Connection*, a bimonthly magazine of news, ideas and information for, by, and about lesbians that has been published bimonthly since 1974. *Margriet Kiers and Kenna Hicks Papers*

Betty Jetter Papers

COLLECTION ID: 1983
COLLECTION DATES: 1981–1988

Active in the Califia women's community, Betty Jetter was also a poet and participant in local lesbian politics. The bulk of the collection (audio and paper) is correspondence between Betty Jetter and Joy Howard and addresses their experiences within the lesbian community, as well as their opinions and thoughts on contemporary political issues such as sadomasochism, lesbian separatism, and pornography. There is also promotional material, photographs, organizational materials, and ephemera from Califia.

Jewish Feminist Conference Records

COLLECTION ID: 1947
COLLECTION DATES: 1971–1983

Modeled on the most famous of the questions from the Passover Seder, the state of purpose of the Jewish Feminist Conference asks, "Why is this conference different from all other conferences?" and responds, "This conference is being organized by Jewish lesbians and Jewish feminists. For many of us the dynamic of being Jewish and lesbian has fueled our energy and provided the impetus for our work." This collection contains documents relating to the planning of two conferences in the San Francisco area in 1982 and 1983. It also includes audiotapes from the conference workshops, as well as flyers and pamphlets from Jewish, feminist, and other lesbian organizations and events in California. The conference packets contain statements on such topics as anti-Semitism, racism, ageism, class and fat oppression, disability and differing cultures within Judaism.

Michelle Johnston Papers

COLLECTION ID: 2200
COLLECTION DATES: 1991–1993

This collection contains transcripts of conversations that took place on the Prodigy internet service provider between Michelle Johnston and four female correspondents. She was an out lesbian, as were several of the other correspondents, although not all. Johnston refers to these transcripts as the presence of "ordinary dykes" in the archives.

Margriet Kiers and Kenna Hicks Papers

COLLECTION ID: 1985
COLLECTION DATES: 1971–1997

Margriet Kiers and Kenna Hicks were both deeply involved with activist organizations in Santa Barbara, as well as national gay, lesbian and feminist organizations. This collection

includes their large periodical collection, as well as personal correspondence and ephemera.

Kim Kralj Papers

COLLECTION ID: 2157
COLLECTION DATES: 1985–1991

Kim Kralj is a lesbian activist, community activist, and art dealer active mainly in Los Angeles, CA. She served on the West Hollywood gay advisory board, and as the President of the Board of the Mazer Archives. The collection consists primarily of agendas, minutes, and general notes of action regarding West Hollywood's recognition and promotion of its gay and lesbian citizens, including information from the Gay and Lesbian Task Force, as well as the Gay and Lesbian Advisory Committee.

Lamis *vs.* Doyle and Sachs Collection of Court Records

COLLECTION ID: 2208
COLLECTION DATES: 1986–1990

Judith M. Doyle was a therapist and was executive director of One in Long Beach, Inc., which runs a gay and lesbian service center. She was a chairwoman of the 1989 AIDS Walk/Long Beach and is one of the founders of the city's annual gay pride parade and festival. This collection spans four years and two separate legal proceedings. A civil suit brought by the plaintiff, Patricia Ann Lamis, against the defendant(s) Judith Manley Doyle and Lilian K. Sachs and the proceedings of the California State Board of Behavioral Science Examiners concerning the eventual loss of Judith Manley Doyle's license to practice for her sexual relationship with her patient Patricia Ann Lamis. The bulk of the collection is made up of depositions and transcripts of proceedings and articles concerning both the licensing and the lawsuit from the *Los Angeles Times*.

Lesbian Catholics Together Records

COLLECTION ID: 1951
COLLECTION DATES: 1986–1992

Dignity USA began in 1969 as an extension of the ministry of Father Patrick X. Nidorf to lesbians and gays. Because the low attendance of women at Dignity functions, a small number of longtime members started to hold women-only liturgies and services. The goal of Lesbian Catholics Together, which began informally in the summer of 1986, focused on expanding the community of Dignity and introducing women to its services. Informally organized, it relied on individual member contributions and volunteer support. With the purpose of "providing a safe and accepting atmosphere in which to socialize, worship and share spiritual journeys," LCT provided monthly liturgies and paraliturgies as well as retreats, monthly support groups, and collaborations with

a benefit for Lesbian Schoolworkers

WHOLE WORKS THEATER
a lesbian theater group

ORIGINAL MUSIC by SIX WOMEN
Christine Bagley   Debbie Saunders
Nancy Henderson   Woody Simmons
Bonnie Lockhart   Nancy Vogal

the LESBIAN SCHOOLWORKER SLIDE SHOW

PEOPLES CULTURIAL CENTER • 721 VALENCIA

WOMEN ONLY • OCT. 27 • 8:30 P.M.

ADMISSION $2.50 $5.00 - SLIDING SCALE o WHEEL CHAIR ACCESSIABLE
CHILD CARE BY RESERVATION 474-7680 EXT. 21 OR 654-9347

Flyer from benefit for Lesbian Schoolworkers at which "Don't Let It Happen Here" slideshow was featured.
Lesbian Schoolworkers Records

other Catholic organizations and gay and lesbian organizations. Collection contains promotional and outreach materials for Lesbian Catholics Together, as well as liturgical and service documentation. Also included are newsletters from the Catholic Conference for Lesbians and some materials from Dignity USA.

Lesbian Love Records

COLLECTION ID: 2207
COLLECTION DATES: 1990

B. Love was a radio personality on KPFK, the listener–sponsored radio station based out of North Hollywood, CA. With content was based on lesbian lives, her shows included episodes on issues such as spirituality, listener call-ins, and interviews. This collection contains ephemera as well as some correspondence and administrative materials.

Lesbian Nurses of Los Angeles Records

COLLECTION ID: 1986
COLLECTION DATES: 1985–1995

The Lesbian Nurses of Los Angeles (LNLA) was formed in 1985 from one RN's desire to identify with other lesbian nurses and to encourage unity within the field. It became a consciousness-raising group for registered nurses (RNs) who shared common ground: "being a woman, being a feminist, and being a lesbian." As part of the group's mission,   combined both social and political energies related to issues on professional nursing, homophobia, discrimination, and identifying as a woman, feminist and lesbian. Meetings, conducted monthly in members' homes and accompanied by a potluck, focused on consciousness raising. They also often included a special topics presentation, guest speaker, and group discussion. LNLA also participated in marches and parades (for instance, annual involvement in the Christopher St. West Parade), and actively collaborated with other community groups.

Collections includes organizational documents such as mission and purpose statements, bylaws, minutes of meetings, attendance records, flyers, newsletters, newspaper articles, and member autobiographies. Also included is information regarding LNLA's 1990 involvement in Suzann Gage *vs.* Santa Monica College, ACLA correspondences, and memorabilia including a scrapbook, t-shirt, and buttons.

Lesbian Schoolworkers Records

COLLECTION ID: 1987
COLLECTION DATES: 1977–1978

With a commitment to "fighting racism, sexism, class and oppression within our own movement and this society,"

the Lesbian Schoolworkers organized in 1977 to defeat the two Briggs Initiatives, Propositions 6 and 7. The organization was among the many to rally against the anti-lesbian and gay initiative, but it was also among the few groups that actively campaigned against the anti-lesbian and pro-death penalty laws, continually pointing out the relationship between Third World oppression and the oppression of all lesbians.

The Lesbian Schoolworkers was organized into three primary committees: Media, Outreach, and Fundraising. With a core group of twenty, and over seventy participants, the group planned many educational activities, sponsored cultural events, and produced leaflets and newsletters aimed at defeating the legislation. Representatives often went before various civic groups, councils, and educational organizations to speak against the measures.

The Schoolworkers are probably best known for their slideshow, "Don't Let It Happen Here." Designed to inform people of the dangers of the Initiatives, it drew together such crucial struggles as affirmative action, abortion rights, death penalty, and oppression of women and lesbians. Amber Hollibaugh, a political activist from San Francisco, traveled throughout small Northern California towns presenting the slideshow and participating in public debates with opposition leaders. Throughout the election fight, the Schoolworkers emphasized that the struggle against Proposition 6 was not about a single issue or a fight for civil rights but "to make it clear to people that we are all suffering at the hands of a common enemy."

The Lesbian Schoolworker Records consist of an organizational history, principles of unity and structure, press releases, newsletters, and photographs. There is also information about both pro and anti-Briggs organizations; a San Francisco Board of Education study on the possibility of including "gay lifestyle" in school curriculum on family and health studies; and the Oregon State Task Force of 1977 report, which collected "information on homosexual men and women in Oregon in order to make recommendations on legislation and administrative policies that would ensure the civil rights of all Oregonians." The records also contain the drafts and final script for the slideshow, "Don't Let It Happen Here," produced by the Schoolworkers to inform people of the dangers of the Briggs Initiatives.

Lesbian Visibility Week Records

COLLECTION ID: 1948
COLLECTION DATES: 1990–1992

Lesbian Visibility Week is a week-long event devoted to raising awareness around lesbian issues and identities, raising the profile of the lesbian community, and celebrating. It is a combination of cultural programming, workshops addressing current and impending needs, awards ceremonies, and social events. Co-sponsored by the West Hollywood Lesbian Visibility Committee and the Los Angeles Gay and Lesbian Center, it is funded in part by the City of West Hollywood.

The West Hollywood Lesbian Visibility Committee

The June L. Mazer Lesbian Collection

WE ARE EVERYWHERE

In celebration of Lesbian Visibility Week in West Hollywood the following events have been scheduled by the June Mazer Lesbian Collection:

MULTICULTURAL POETRY READING

On Friday, July 13, 1990 at 8:00 p.m. in the Council Chambers (downstairs), 626 N. Robertson Boulevard, a Multicultural Poetry Reading will be held featuring:

> **Aleida Rodríguez:** a Cuban-born lesbian poet and prose writer. Widely published, she is also the recipient of a National Endowment for the Arts Creative Writing Fellowship.

> **Bia Lowe:** a Los Angeles-based writer who has been published in anthologies and literary magazines.

> **Mariah L. Richardson:** a young African-American poet/actress living in Los Angeles. A fresh voice for the '90s.

> **Sophia Corleone:** a Sicilian-American lesbian living in Silver Lake. Sometimes she writes poetry but now mostly autobiographical vignettes on growing up gay. Her main influences in life have been Marilyn Monroe, Rita Hayworth and Betty Boop. She's not kidding.

Come early so you can spend time viewing an exhibit of materials from the Collection that has been arranged in the Council Chamber. Refreshments. No charge. Donations to the June Mazer Lesbian Collection are appreciated.

MARILYN MURPHY TO READ

On Sunday, July 15, 1990 from 1:30 - 3:30 p.m., LA's Marilyn Murphy, activist and *Lesbian News* columnist, will read from her latest writings at the Mazer Collection, 626 N. Robertson Boulevard. Refreshments will be served. Donations to the Collection are welcome. Please call to reserve a space (213/659-2478).

LESBIAN EXHIBIT

Be sure to come to the West Hollywood Park Auditorium (Heritage Pavilion, 647 N. San Vicente) on June 23rd & 24th during the Lesbian & Gay Pride Festival to see the special exhibition from the June Mazer Lesbian Collection. This is a wonderful opportunity to learn about the Collection and to get involved!

"We are Everywhere" announcement for the Mazer Archives' activities for Lesbian Visibility Week in 1990. *Lesbian Visibility Week Records*

"Dykes and Their Dogs"
PET SHOW

Saturday, July 14th

at
West Hollywood Park
647 N. San Vicente Blvd.

REGISTRATION: Noon   ENTRY FEE: $3.00
SHOW: 12:30 P.M. to 2:30 P.M.

CATEGORIES

- ★ **Fastest Eater**
- ★ **Best Dog Trick**
- ★ **Best Butch Dog Dressed as a Femme**
- ★ **Best Femme Dog Dressed as a Butch**
- ★ **Dog That Looks Most Like Their Owner**
- ★ **Best Kisser**

WIN SOME FABULOUS PRIZES FOR YOUR DOG!
A Trainer Will Give A Demonstration of Dog Obedience

Co-sponsored by the City of West Hollywood's Lesbian and Gay Advisory Council
and the West Hollywood Marketing Corporation for Lesbian Visibility Week 1990.

"Dykes and their Dogs" Pet Show was popular event during Lesbian Visibility Week in 1990. *Lesbian Visibility Week Records*

(WeHo LVC) was established in 1989 to bring awareness to lesbians living and loving in West Hollywood, CA, one of the largest lesbian communities in America. WeHo LVC endeavors to bring justice where injustices are being carried out in the lesbian community and to act as a resource for women in need.

This collection includes correspondence, notes, promotional materials, display boards and photographs all centered around the planning and execution of the annual event. Although the collection is dominated by materials from 1990, Lesbian Visibility Week continued to have a strong presence throughout the 1990s and 2000s.

Robin Ruth Linden Papers

COLLECTION ID: 1957
COLLECTION DATES: 1976–1984

Robin Ruth Linden is a writer and sociologist whose research has explored women's health, the politics of technomedicine, the Holocaust, reflexive ethnography, and life histories. She received the Helen Hooven Santmyer Prize in women's studies and was the Associate Dean of the Graduate School for Holistic Studies at John F. Kennedy University in Orinda, CA.

Her major works include *Against Sadomasochism: A Radical Feminist Analysis* (editor), *Making Stories, Making Selves: Feminist Reflections on the Holocaust* (author), and *AIDS on the Ground: Service Learning in a Global Epidemic* (coauthored with Carolyn Laub).

Linden also founded the Holocaust Media Project with Lani Silver in 1983. It became the Bay Area Holocaust Oral History Project whose mission is to gather oral life histories of Holocaust survivors, liberators, rescuers, and eyewitnesses. The Project is developing and maintaining a catalogue database for public use.

Linden was also involved with Women Against Violence in Pornography and Media (WAVPM), a radical feminist anti-pornography activist group based in San Francisco, and an influential force in the larger feminist anti-pornography movement of the late 1970s and 1980s. The feminist sex, or porn, wars of the 1970s and 1980s saw anti-pornography feminists opposed to sex-positive feminists and led to deep divisions in the movement.

Linden was also involved in distribution for Olivia Records, a collective founded in 1973 to record and market women's music. Olivia Records drew criticism from a transphobic portion of the lesbian community, as documented in the collection, because Sandy Stone, a transgender academic theorist, media theorist, author and performance artist, was the organization's sound engineer.

The collection contains working notes, manuscripts and drafts from *Against Sadomasochism* and materials from the establishment of the Women's Studies program at UC Santa Cruz, and financial and distribution information for Olivia Records. Notes, release forms and funding for the production of *Feminism and Science,* a video produced by Linden, are also included, as are documents relating to the Feminism and the Philosophy of Science Conference, which served as inspiration for the video. Letters, reviews, and information relating to Mary Daly's feminist theology and ethics courses at Boston College, as well as other articles and essays relating to a broad range of feminist topics are also represented.

Los Angeles Women's Community Chorus Records

COLLECTION ID: 2171
COLLECTION DATES: 1977–1990

The Los Angeles Women's Community Chorus is a Los Angeles based nonprofit chorus of and for women. Established in 1976, the chorus intended to raise feminist and political consciousness by presenting choral music of all genres (historical, contemporary, classical, folk, popular, and ethnic) for women, by women, and about women. Over the next decade and a half, the collective sought to foster an environment of openness and positivity while encouraging excellence in musicianship. Its members were committed to combating discrimination based not only on gender, but on sexuality, race, age and disability.

Starting from a small group of founding members (Carol Petracca, Joelyn Grippo, Lynn Wilson, Anna Rubin, Silvia Kohan, Faye Haines, and Sue Fink), the Chorus soon grew to between sixty to a hundred members. The group presented a fully produced concert annually in May or June and generally held a benefit dance in February to raise funds. The LAWCC was also funded, in part, by grants from the City of Los Angeles. In addition to the annual concerts, the Chorus performed with a significant number of other organizations at events throughout its season. These included the Southern California Women for Understanding (SCWU), National Organization for Women (NOW), Women against Violence against Women (WAVAW), Gay Atheists League of America (GALA), Connexxus Women's Center/Centro de Mujeres, the Gay and Lesbian Center (GLCSC), Christopher Street West. The LAWCC's network of collaboration also included other choir organizations, such as the American Choral Directory Association, the Choral Directing Guild, and the Gay Men's Chorus, and a number of lesbian and feminist publications and organizations, including Hotwire, Lesbian News, Lesbian Central, and Handywoman Collective.

In the spirit of community, the Chorus held open rehearsals every season and included music composed and arranged by its members. A system was set up that would allow for a safe space for productive critical feedback. Music was included from outside the classical Western canon, and printed materials in programs and songbooks included Spanish and Braille translations. Childcare was regularly provided at rehearsals and performances. As evidenced in meeting minutes and other materials in this collection, the values of the Chorus were constantly negotiated as it grew in size and organizational complexity over its years of existence. Discussions about how to keep open rehearsals while also preparing to put on a professional, fully produced annual show that required a regular time commitment from its members continued into the Chorus' later years. The group constantly negotiated political ideologies and musical professionalism, with the aim of not sacrificing either.

In 1986, the Chorus produced a major recording project for its tenth anniversary (despite significant financial and logistical hurdles) and saw the departure of Sue Fink, conductor and general leader of the Chorus for its first ten years, who was replaced by Kay Erdwin. Despite changes in leadership, committee members, and overall participation, a core group of women kept the Chorus running from its inception to 1990. A twentieth-anniversary reunion event in 1997 brought many of its former members back to Los Angeles for a celebration of the Chorus and its history of feminist consciousness-raising and community building in Los Angeles through music.

This collection contains administrative and documentary material recording the functioning and public presentations. The administrative records, including meeting minutes, committee papers, programs, songbooks and tickets from the Chorus' annual shows, and publicity and fundraising materials, cover a twenty-year span from 1977 to its twentieth-anniversary reunion in 1997. The collection also contains photographs, albums, and audiovisual material of concerts and social gatherings, as well as copies of the tenth-anniversary album.

Bunny MacCulloch Papers

COLLECTION ID: 1959
COLLECTION DATES: 1928–1989

Nancy (Bunny) MacCulloch (*shown at left with June Mazer*) was a lifelong activist and community partner, serving as an active participant and board member to several organizations including the Southern California Women for Understanding, Connexxus, and the West Coast Lesbian Collections. She was also an accomplished film editor and avid collector.

MacCulloch joined the Southern California Women for Understanding (SCWU) in 1978, serving as their archivist, co-editing the newsletter and serving a two-year term as secretary. She met June Mazer, who became the love of her life, at a meeting of the SCWU. Together they adopted the West Coast Lesbian Collections of memorabilia, which had been founded in San Francisco and was looking for a home. Before she passed away, MacCulloch put a tremendous amount of effort into

cataloging the collections and acquiring materials. Eventually it was put under the umbrella of the International Gay and Lesbian Archives, sponsored by Connexxus, and named the June L. Mazer Collection (now called the June L. Mazer Lesbian Archives).

MacCulloch received the Community Service Award from SCWU in March, 1988, and a proclamation from the City of West Hollywood on May 7, 1989. The acceptance of this award was her last public appearance.

Spanning professional activities and affiliations, activist and community organizations, personal papers and historical papers, the collection represents MacCulloch's work in film editing as well as her participation in the SCWU, the Mazer Archives, and other activist organizations in Los Angeles. It also includes audio recordings of MacCulloch in both personal and official capacities.

Barbara Macdonald Papers

COLLECTION ID: 2159
COLLECTION DATES: 1979–2003

Barbara Anne (Charles) Macdonald, social worker, lesbian feminist activist, and author, grew up in the vicinity of La Habra, CA. At the age of fifteen, she left home permanently and began supporting herself as a domestic worker in Long Beach, CA. In 1930, Macdonald married Elmo Davis. The marriage lasted five years. She attended Long Beach Junior College (1931–1932) and Santa Ana Junior College (1932–1937), where she was nearly expelled for being a lesbian, and UC Berkeley (1938–1940). She paid for her education by working as a stunt parachute jumper, about which she was the subject of numerous articles in the *Santa Ana Register*, which called her "intrepid and daring." She married John Macdonald in 1941, but the marriage was very brief.

After leaving UC Berkeley, Macdonald worked at the WPA Housing Authority in Vallejo, CA. From 1950 to 1953, she attended the University of Washington, where she received a B.A. and an M.S.W. Upon graduation she moved to Wenatchee, WA, and worked as a supervisor for Child Welfare Services. In 1957 she moved to Morgantown, WV, and commuted to the University of Pennsylvania, where she worked on a third-year certificate in psychiatric social work. She worked as a clinical social worker in pediatrics at the University of Maryland, and taught at the medical school. She lived in Baltimore, MD, from 1964 to 1967 and worked as a school social worker in the Baltimore public schools. During this time, she took up sailing and bought a sailboat named "Mighty Mouse." In 1967 she moved to Connecticut, where she worked as a consultant for the Bureau of Pupil Personnel and Special Education for the state. Macdonald and her companion Ethel Weeden, also a social worker, took a year's leave to travel the country in a Volkswagen bus. They followed that with a trip by freighter to Asia.

Macdonald retired as a social worker in 1974. That same year, she took a feminist writing workshop at Goddard-Cambridge Graduate School in Cambridge, MA. The workshop was taught by Cynthia Rich, who became Macdonald's domestic partner. They were together for twenty-six years. Mcdonald died June 15, 2000.

Macdonald's work appeared frequently in such lesbian and feminist publications as *Equal Times*, *Lesbian Ethics*, *Ms.*, *New Directions*, *New Women's Times*, *Sinister Wisdom*, and *Sojourner*. In 1980, she covered the UN Mid-Decade Conference on Women in Copenhagen for *Equal Times*. In 1983, Rich and Macdonald co-authored *Look Me in the Eye: Old Women, Aging and Ageism*. The book, which appeared in expanded editions in 1991 and 2001, combined her personal experiences of ageism with groundbreaking lesbian feminist theory. Named one of thirty-five classics of second-wave feminism by *Ms Magazine*, it is widely anthologized for courses in women's and gender studies.

A frequent speaker at lesbian and feminist organizations, universities, and organizations of social workers nationally and internationally, including the UN Conference on Women at Huairou, China, in 1995, she was the keynote speaker at the National Lesbian Conference in Atlanta in 1991 and gave a plenary address at the National Women's Studies Conference in 1985. In 1987, she served on the planning committee and gave the keynote address for the first West Coast Conference of Old Lesbians. Out of this conference came Old Lesbians Organizing for Change, a national organization seeking to end the discrimination experienced by old women. The collection contains published and unpublished talks, drafts, notes, ephemera, promotional material, and publisher's correspondence.

Maud's Project Records

COLLECTION ID: 2206
COLLECTION DATES: 1986–1993

Maud's was a lesbian bar in San Francisco, CA, that opened in 1966 and closed its doors in 1989. The film sets the historical, cultural, and social context for the opening of Maud's, including the formation of the Daughters of Bilitis in 1955, the development of lesbian community and the need for alternatives to gay men's bars, which were the targets of police raids throughout the 1950s. Rikki Streicher (1926–1994), owner/operator of Maud's and Amelia's (also a lesbian bar) throughout its existence, was a leader in San Francisco's gay rights movement, and a creator of the Federation of Gay Games. This collection concerns the release and making of the documentary *Last Call at Maud's*. Directed by Paris Poirier and produced by Poirier and Karen Kisshe, the documentary uses archival documents and first-person interviews to trace the history and decline of Maud's, as well as the AIDS crisis and the assassination of Harvey Milk. The materials include press packets for the film, some research materials used during the making of the film, and documentation concerning the premiere of the film at the Pacific Design Center in September of 1993.

June L. Mazer Papers

COLLECTION ID: 2136
COLLECTION DATES: 1929–1988

June Mazer was editor/publisher of the SCWU newsletter as well as a member of the organization's board. *Southern California Women for Understanding Records*

Born in Baltimore, MD, in 1929, June L. Mazer received her Bachelor of Arts from Goucher College in 1949, where she served as the editor of the college newspaper. In 1952, June earned the title O.T.R. (Occupational Therapist Registered) through the School of Occupational Therapy at the University of Pennsylvania, Philadelphia. In 1964, Mazer received her Master of Arts from the Catholic University of America in Washington, DC, with a focus in drama and social work. These educational experiences—combined with her tenures at the Children's Experimental Theatre in Baltimore, the Center for the Healing Arts in Los Angeles, and the California Institute of Psychodrama in Los Angeles—led her to the practice of psychodrama therapy at several different medical institutions throughout the country. During this time, Mazer also contributed articles on her work to many professional journals.

In 1970 she moved to Los Angeles, CA, and soon became active in the lesbian activist community. She joined the Board of Directors of the Southern California Women/Whitman Radcliffe Foundation and remained active when it branched off and became the Southern California Women for Understanding, an educational nonprofit dedicated to the enhancement of quality of life for lesbians everywhere.

In 1979, Mazer met Bunny MacCulloch and they became lovers. The couple were passionate and consistent believers in the preservation of lesbian history. Together they were involved in, supported, or belonged to a number of progressive organizations including the American Civil Liberties Union, Connexxus Women's Center, the Gay and Lesbian Press Association, the International Gay and Lesbian Archives (IGLA), the National Gay and Lesbian Task Force, the Lesbian Rights Project, and the Southern California Women for Understanding.

In 1985, Mazer was diagnosed with cancer and died on January 16, 1987. To commemorate her commitment to lesbian activism and historical preservation, the archives are renamed the June L. Mazer Lesbian Archives.

SAN DIEGO

PROTEST

THE MYTH CALIFORNIA "BEAUTY" CONTEST

JUNE 15TH MON. 1987

7:00 P.M.

PEACEFUL PROTEST

CIVIC CENTER 2ND + "C" ST.

"TAKE YOUR BUSINESS OFF WOMEN'S BODIES"

"SCHOLARSHIPS FOR GOOD MINDS NOT GOOD LEGS"

INFO. CENTRAL 224-7530 - MEETINGS EVERY WEDS. 7PM - 281-4760

Flyer for "The Myth California 'Beauty'" Contest. *Diane Germain Papers*

This collection contains Mazer's personal, professional and activist materials, including photographs, journals, correspondence, artworks, astrology readings, ephemera, identification documents, and other personal materials. A portion of the collection is made up of professional literature in the field of occupational therapy, and her publications on psychodrama and innovations in occupational therapy. Also included are newsletters for the Southern California Women for Understanding, of which Mazer was an editor, as well as clippings of articles and reviews by Mazer. The bulk of the collection deals with Mazer's illness and death, including medical information, documentation of daily habits and feelings, letters of condolence, and diaries, as well as obituaries and articles about Mazer published after her death.

Mazer Collection of Audio Materials

COLLECTION ID: 2230
COLLECTION DATES: 1970–1999

This collection of 555 audio recordings features nearly seven hundred hours of unique and historically valuable audio. Persons include: Judy Grahn, Margaret (Peg) Cruikshank, Judy Freespirit, June L. Mazer, Bunny MacCulloch, Del Martin, Phyllis Lyon, Kitty Tsui, Eloise Klein Healy, Anne Sexton, Lillian Faderman, Liz Maines, and others. The content of the material includes recordings of conferences, workshops, meetings, performances, radio broadcasts, interviews, and oral histories concerning topics such as homosexuality, women's health, politics, women in history, feminism, racism, discrimination, literature, and music.

The digitized collections present a range of topics with a variety of hosts and speakers. From music recordings to scholarly talks to small group medical information sessions, the audio collection captures the culture, diversity, politics, scholarship, and activism that feminist and lesbian communities have produced throughout the last fifty years. The tapes are a reflection of the significant amount of activism that women were involved with in Los Angeles and California throughout the latter half of the twentieth century.

Of particular note is the "June L. Mazer and Bunny MacCulloch Interviews etc. (1981–1990)" set, which includes interviews with Mazer and MacCulloch concerning the Southern California Women for Understanding (SCWU), the Mazer Archives, Mazer's death, and lesbian culture in the San Francisco Bay Area. The audio recordings provide great insight into the life and work of both Mazer and MacCulloch, who were prominent figures in the lesbian community of the West Coast. The women conducted interviews with scholars and other experts on lesbian culture and history and were also the subjects of interviews. The collection includes a recording of the Jewish memorial service that honored the life and work of Mazer after her death in 1987.

Mazer Collection of Video Materials

COLLECTION ID: 2231
COLLECTION DATES: 1980–2005

The collection of video materials includes these series: Ester Bentley Collection; Califia (14 August 1983 to 21 August 1983); Califia; Diane Germain; Curation Series: Angela Brinskele; Maud's Project; Old Lesbians Organizing for Change; and Southern California Women for Understanding.

Deborah McCormick Papers

COLLECTION ID: 2191
COLLECTION DATES: 1979–1989

Deborah McCormick and Janet Rauch were founding mothers of the weekly women's music program "Face the Music" on public station WFBE-FM in Flint, MI. The program was active throughout the 1980s, ending when the station was sold in 1997. The program focused on lesbian and women's music, featuring both mainstream and alternative musicians. This collection contains press materials, programs and publicity information for individual women performers as well as large scale women's music and performance festivals between 1979 and 1989.

Ruth McGuire Papers

COLLECTION ID: 2194
COLLECTION DATES: 1961–1985

Ruth McGuire was one of the cofounders of The Women's Foundation of California, a publicly supported foundation focused on human trafficking intervention and prevention, lesbian and transgender rights, environmental health, criminal justice work, and campaigns to build women's economic security. McGuire was also a member of the Daughters of Bilitis, the first lesbian civil and political rights organization in the U.S. In 1968 she published a short story in the lesbian publication *The Ladder* titled "The Intake Interview," which dealt with lesbian identity in the context of the mental health profession, from the perspectives of both patient and health care provider. Collection contains referrals, correspondence and preliminary reports from several different practitioners of psychoanalytic techniques.

Elaine Mikels Papers

COLLECTION ID :   1954
COLLECTION DATES: 1977–1984

Elaine Mikels was born in 1921 in Los Angeles, CA, where she spent much of her early life. Even though her family was Jewish, she attended Flintridge, a Catholic boarding school. Through different mediums, Mikels has spoken about her early relationships with women who identified as straight

Our OWN Summer 1980

Summer 1980 of issue of *Our OWN*, newsletter of the Older Women's Network. *Elaine Mikels Papers*

and later went on to get married. Similarly to other closeted women living in the 1940s, she had little concept of how to deal with her own relationships, much less build community through shared interests. During this period she suffered from depression and was hospitalized for severe episodes.

After World War II ended, Mikels worked in Germany with the Quakers through the Department of State, but she was expelled from the program because of her psychiatric record. Returning to the U.S. and settled briefly in New York, she travelled for the next several years throughout Europe and the Middle East. In 1951 she settled in San Francisco and pursued social work. In San Francisco she became active in the Mattachine Society and ONE magazine. It was also during this period, in 1959, that she established the Conard House. The Conard House was the first halfway house in San Francisco, specifically conceived as a transitional community for people with mental illness who were returning to San Francisco from Napa State Hospital.

In the late 1960s, Mikels became, in her own estimation, political. She joined the anti-war movement, joined lesbian-feminist communities in Oregon, and participated in peace action with lesbians in North Carolina. In 1976, she founded the Older Women's Network in order to bring older lesbian feminists together to share resources and achieve their activist goals. She would go on to participate in similar groups, and helped to found the group Older Lesbians Organizing for Change. Mikels also worked on *Feminary*, a newsletter published by a women's collective in Durham. Began as *Feminist Journal for the South*, the newsletter was funded through the University of North Carolina at Chapel

Making Invisible Histories Visible

Hill, where it was mimeographed by the group involved. With the inception of the Triangle Area Lesbian Feminists, the journal shifted focus somewhat and took on more of a lesbian-feminist bent.

The collection includes photographs taken by Mikels of lesbian activist gatherings, lesbian social gatherings and sports clubs, and lesbian writing groups. Self-published newsletters also document these events. The collection contains over two hundred hand processed photographs, materials related to the publication of *Just Lucky I Guess: From Closet Lesbian to Radical Dyke,* and a copy of the final published version. Also included are personal papers, journals, correspondence, and other personal materials. The pictures contained in the Mikels collection of *Feminary* writers, producers and supporters reflect the publication's developing political imperative and changes in its content. Also represented in the collection are photographs documenting the Women's Pentagon Action, a two-thousand woman protest that surrounded the Pentagon in 1981. Although Mikels eventually settled in Santa Fe, NM, most of her photographic collection represents her life in Oregon and North Carolina.

Jean Miller Papers

COLLECTION ID: 2139
COLLECTION DATES: 1964–1980

An early participant in the women's liberation movement as a member of Women of the Free Future and Women in Solidarity, Jean Lewis Miller was lesbian feminist activist in the Bay Area. She worked part-time as an employee of the Berkeley Public Library. In 1971 she was fired for writing a article in the *Berkeley Post* exposing sexism and racism in the library. After twenty-five women marched on the Board of Directors meeting, she was reinstated and dedicated herself to serving women's needs within the library through her self-created Women's Project. This group was later discontinued by the library, after her formation of the Berkeley Women's Affirmative Action Union. At another public protest, Miller became the first person arrested at a meeting of the Berkeley City Council. Thereafter, she endured a nine-day hunger strike in Santa Rita and was jailed a second time. Then, she was fired and jailed a third time. Although she was acquitted, she was jailed for contempt of court. Miller filed a lawsuit in federal court charging sex discrimination and political retaliation in 1974. Years later, the case was dismissed. In 1980, Miller died after a two-month battle with cancer.

The collection consists of documents relating to Miller's political struggles with the city of Berkeley over affirmative action and sex and race discrimination. Included are legal documents, suffragist literature, college research papers,

letters to her son, materials relating to Inez Garcia (an Hispanic woman who became a cause célèbre of the feminist movement when in 1974 she was charged with the murder of a man who had raped her), and unpublished manuscripts on motherhood and women's sexuality.

Marilyn Murphy Papers

COLLECTION ID: 2226
COLLECTION DATES: 1980–1995

Marilyn Murphy was a longtime lesbian activist and author. She had a long-running column in *Lesbian News* in 1982 titled "Lesbian Logic," and a selection of her columns appeared in the 1991 book, *Are You Girls Traveling Alone?* This collection contains personal papers, correspondence, and a copy of *Are You Girls Traveling Alone?* She was an active member of the organization Old Lesbians Organizing for Change and is survived by her partner, Irene Weiss.

Cheryl Nassar Papers

COLLECTION ID: 2227
COLLECTION DATES: 1960–1995

Cheryl Nassar was a photographer and active member of the lesbian activist community in Southern California. Nassar was born in 1944 and grew up in Pennsylvania. She received a Bachelor's degree in English Literature from the University of Pittsburgh. Throughout the 1980s, she was active in women's rights as well as gay and lesbian rights organizations. She was the official photographer for many of the gay pride events throughout Southern California. She was also an avid collector of porcelain dolls. This collection contains photographs, videotapes, and ephemera from lesbian and gay pride events throughout the region.

National Gay and Lesbian Task Force Records

COLLECTION ID: 2205
COLLECTION DATES: 1980–1989

The National Gay and Lesbian Task Force is an American nonprofit organization focused on building, supporting and educating a grassroots community around LGBT rights and causes. It was founded in 1973 by Dr. Howard Brown, Dr. Bruce Voeller, Reverend Robert Carter, and Dr. Frank Kameny. Focused on supporting the grassroots power of the lesbian, gay, bisexual and transgender community, the National Gay and Lesbian Task Force has offices in multiple cities and engages with a range of activities and outreach.

The NGLTF runs Creating Change, the National Conference on LGBT Equality, and operates a Policy Institute, a thinktank that conducts social science research, policy analysis, strategy development, public education, and advocacy.

This collection contains organizational documents and

ALL LESBIANS URGED TO ATTEND

It's About Time !!!
A

National Lesbian Feminist Organization

Dealing with the oppression of Lesbians in all its manifestations including but not limited to discrimination based on sexual preference, sex, race, class, age and physical disability;

Educating Lesbians and the general public as to the social, political, and economic and racial oppression of Lesbians;

To develop Lesbian culture.

TWO OPEN MEETINGS:

For the purpose of information sharing and discussion.

June 7 at 8 p.m. at the Emma Goldman Clinic for Women
715 N. Dodge St.

June 13 at 7:30 p.m. at the Women's Resource and Action Center
130 Madison Ave.

Flyer announcing the effort to create a national lesbian feminist organization. *National Lesbian Feminist Organization Records*

research materials from the Los Angeles office of the National Gay and Lesbian Task Force during the 1980s. Also included is some correspondence as well as surveys and data collection projects related to HIV/AIDS public service availability and vulnerable populations.

National Lesbian Conference Records

COLLECTION ID: 2202
COLLECTION DATES: 1989–1991

The National Lesbian Conference became a concept after the attendees from the U.S. at an international lesbian conference in 1986 felt that they had no unified voice because of a lack of a national lesbian agenda. In 1988, a few lesbians met in Washington, DC, to plan a national lesbian conference. Subsequently, planning meetings were held in North Carolina, Oregon, and Missouri. Meetings operated by modified consensus. Consensus and parity (defined as 50% lesbians of color, 20% disabled lesbians and 5% old lesbians) were of prime importance. The full steering committee, with over 100 seats to represent many different interest groups, was never fully seated.

The National Lesbian Conference was the first and only of its kind, attempting to set a national lesbian activist agenda. The event took place in Atlanta, GA, in 1991 and drew over twenty-five hundred registered attendees. The gathering included one full day of caucuses, five plenaries, four mornings of anti-oppression training, and nearly three hundred workshops. Although the goal was to decide collectively on a national lesbian agenda, it remained elusive. The conference became fertile ground for intra-organizational conversations about representation and the political process, but a fair amount of strife and dissent plagued much of the conversation. This collection contains some planning materials as well as a conference program and news coverage of the conference.

National Lesbian Feminist Organization Records

COLLECTION ID: 1944
COLLECTION DATES: 1978–1979

The National Lesbian Feminist Organization (NLFO) was founded in 1978 as a grassroots organization in order to "act on a feminist platform which deals with the oppression of lesbians in all its manifestations, including but not limited to discrimination based on sexual preference, sex, race, age, class, and physical disability. There is a need to achieve equal rights and legal protections for all lesbians...a need for developing lesbian culture." An ad-hoc committee formed in Los Angeles and took responsibility for planning of a national convention to be held in July of 1978. A nationally based steering committee was selected at the convention, whose responsibility was to guide the organization through the first crucial months.

As a grassroots organization concerned with

Flyer for conference on "Women and Global Corporations: Work-Roles & Resistance." *National Lesbian Feminist Organization Records*

accountability, the NLFO committed itself to fighting racism and classism both inside and outside the organization. The group called for a "minimum of 50% of all the women involved in the level of planning and decision making to be women of color of various backgrounds and 50% of all white women of various class backgrounds." Membership was open to all lesbians and women identified women who agreed with the purpose of the organization. The structure of the NLFO consisted of local memberships known as the "locals," whose representatives were sent to state and national conventions. The Los Angeles chapter was named the Alice Paul chapter.

This collection contains an organizational history, founding convention notes, correspondence, ad hoc and steering committee memos, financial statements, and newsletters. Also contained is information on local and state chapters, resources, and lesbian rights marches. Additional materials highlight behind-the-scenes efforts to organize local chapters, the formation of the Lesbians of Color Caucus, and disagreements over the credibility of "representative organizations."

Sass Nielson Papers

COLLECTION ID: 2162
COLLECTION DATES: 1974–1975

Sass Nielson worked at Walt Disney Studios in Burbank, CA, throughout the 1990s. As a young woman, she was kicked out of the military for being a lesbian. She also wrote fiction. Her advocacy work, growing out of the group Hollywood Supports (a nonprofit organization promoting awareness of AIDS and gay issues) concerned the extension of health benefits for same-sex partners as well as organizing around lesbian and gay issues in the workplace. In 1992, she successfully organized the formation of the Lesbian and Gay United Employees (LEAGUE). This collection includes research, correspondence, and materials related to gay and lesbian issues, including information from activist organizations and publications that treat the issue historically.

Pat Nordell Papers

COLLECTION ID: 2143
COLLECTION DATES: 1957–2000

Born in 1932 and raised in Wheaton, IL, Patricia Nordell is a Los Angeles–based lesbian sports coach and photographer. As is evidenced in the collection, she was a star athlete and popular personality through her high school years at Wheaton Community High School, from which she graduated in 1950. Nordell stayed in the Midwest after high school, playing amateur and intramural sports in Wheaton and Chicago. She excelled in a number of sports, including basketball, volleyball, baseball, and bowling.

Nordell completed a teaching degree at the Illinois State Normal University in June 1957 and continued her college education at the University of Arizona at Tucson, receiving a

Pat Nordell (sitting on car hood) and friends. Pat Nordell Papers

Bachelor of Science in 1960. She continued her engagement with sports, playing intramural volleyball and basketball.

She moved to Southern California in 1960 to start her teaching career at Coachella Valley Union High, where she taught Physical Education for three years. By 1972, she had moved to Los Angeles and began teaching at Westchester High School (WHS), where she continued for the remaining sixteen years of her career. Nordell coached Varsity Girls' Basketball, Girls' Softball, and Women's Track and Field from 1973 onwards, leading the basketball team to their first-ever California State championship win a few years later. In 1980, she received recognition from both the California Coaches Association and the National High School Athletic Coaches Association as Track & Field "Coach of the Year" for her outstanding record at WHS: a 45-1 dual meet record including six Western league titles, two LA city titles (1977 and 1979), and a State championship (1979). The same year, Nordell started coaching Men's Track and Field at WHS, making her one of the first women to coach a men's athletic team in Los Angeles.

Perhaps because of her own experience playing sports, Nordell was highly invested in combating gender discrimination in sports. Fighting against the notion that girls shouldn't play sports because it was "unfeminine," she was an advocate for women teachers and coaches, whom she felt were trivialized. She publically spoke out against gender bias in pay scales and, most importantly, initiated a law suit in the 1970s against the Los Angeles Unified School District for equal pay for women coaches, which she won in the late 1980s.

With its array of scrapbooks and photographs, this collection gives a comprehensive view of Nordell's professional and personal life. The scrapbooks provide a comprehensive record of her career in sports, teaching, and coaching, while the photographs provide a view into Nordell's private life,

If you know a **Lesbian Over 60**, *tell her about this event!*

If you are a Lesbian planning on passing 60 someday, *help us pave the way.*

and

If you're a **Lesbian Over 60**, *join us at this event:*

First West Coast Old Lesbian Conference and Celebration

April 24, 25, and 26
Dominguez Hills College
Carson, California
(Los Angeles Area)

Read more about it on the back of this page,
and for more information,
or for registration materials,
use the registration slip below,
or phone:

Bay Area Support Committee
(415) 528-0018

- -

To: **West Coast Celebration, c/o P.O. Box 31787, San Francisco, CA 94131**

☐ Please send registration information and materials to the address below.

☐ I'm enclosing a contribution in support of the conference, and to keep it
available to women over 60 at all income levels: $ _____

My name: _____

Address: _____

City: _____ State: _____ Zip: _____

Flyer announcing the First West Coast Old Lesbian Conference and Celebration. *Old Lesbians Organizing for Change Records*

especially following her retirement in 1988. They document relationships, Nordell's love for outdoor activity, and her involvement in gay and lesbian communities in Southern California.

Old Lesbians Organizing for Change Records

COLLECTION ID: 2203
COLLECTION DATES: 1986–1992

Old Lesbians Organizing for Change (OLOC) is a national organization for lesbians over the age of 60. Using education and public discourse, its core mission is to combat ageism and increase visibility for older lesbians. After the publication of Barbara Macdonald and Cynthia Rich's *Look Me in the Eye: Old Women, Aging and Ageism* by a group of lesbians were inspired and empowered to organize the First West Coast Conference and Celebration for Old Lesbians in Southern California. The event was held at the California State University, Dominguez Hills Campus in Carson, CA, in April of 1987. Out of those who attended this conference and its follow-up in 1989, a group of sixteen decided to meet to form an organization. At the first organizational meeting, a name was chosen, a statement of purpose drafted, tasks assigned, a coordinator designated, and future meetings were scheduled. The Old Lesbian Organizing Committee (later renamed Old Lesbians Organizing for Change) had begun.

Participation was strictly limited to lesbians 60 years of age and older. However, the organization has always welcomed the support of younger lesbians while maintaining the need for separate space. OLOC quickly created a newsletter with a national reach and began enrolling members. Early efforts were concentrated on developing educational materials on ageism, using consciousness-raising techniques. These materials were pooled and published in *The Facilitator's Handbook: Confronting Ageism: Consciousness Raising for Lesbians 60 and Over.*

OLOC took a strong and highly visible part in the National Lesbian Conference in Atlanta, GA, in 1991, as well as at the march on Washington in 1993. By 1992, OLOC sought and gained nonprofit status, incorporating in the state of Texas, and achieving tax-exempt status in 1994. In 1996, OLOC held its first National Gathering, on the campus of the University of Minnesota in Minneapolis. In 1999, its second gathering was held in San Francisco, CA. The third was in 2002, again in Minnesota. Conferences are now held every other year. OLOC continues to produce a quarterly newsletter called *The OLOC Reporter*, coordinate biennial gatherings, participate in the Old Lesbian Oral Herstory Project, and produce a line of age-positive, women-friendly greeting cards.

The majority of the materials in the collection deal with the West Coast Conference and Celebration, its planning and programming. Also included is correspondence between members and the steering committee.

Terri de la Peña Papers

COLLECTION ID: 1960
COLLECTION DATES: 1988–1996

Terri de La Peña is a novelist, short story writer, and children's book author whose writings deal with complex issues of identity, homophobia, assimilation and resistance focusing on the lives of Chicana lesbians. A fifth-generation Californian, Mary Theresa de la Peña was born on February 20, 1947, in Santa Monica. Her father, Joaquin de la Peña, was a tire repair foreman; her mother, Juanita Escobedo, owned a beauty shop. De la Peña was educated in Santa Monica parochial schools and at Santa Monica Community College. She is a self-taught writer. She wrote her first novel, *Margins*, while employed as an academic affairs assistant with the College of Letters and Science at UCLA. The majority of her work is in short story form. Her narratives revolve around the myriad cultural and social issues facing Chicana lesbians such as a search for identity, cultural assimilation, class consciousness, historical awareness, internal and external racism, homophobia and visibility.

Collection contains materials related to the creation, dissemination, publication and revision of both fictional and nonfictional works. The bulk is made up of drafts of *Margins*. The collection includes correspondence, contractual information, promotional materials, drafts, and notes.

Margaret A. Porter Papers

COLLECTION ID: 1906
COLLECTION DATES: 1900–1989

Born in Milwaukee, WI, Margaret A. Porter (*shown above*) was a distinguished poet and translator of French poetry. She began writing poetry at the age of 12. At the same age, Porter observed that she was different but did not yet know words to describe herself as a lesbian. While in college at Marquette University, she first published under the name Pierre E. Renet, a name she used to write poetry from the

Statement of Purpose

OUR PURPOSE in calling together old Lesbians, 60 and over, is to explore who we are, name our oppression, celebrate all that we represent, and make our presence a force in the women's movement.

We have invented our own lives. We have expanded and liberated the meaning of being a woman. We are inventing our own aging. We want to share our discoveries.

We want to analyze our experience of ageism, which has been so little defined, know how to name it and resist it. Society calls us "old" behind our backs while calling us "older" to our faces. We refuse the lie that it is shameful to be an old woman.

We want to celebrate our differences and affirm the diversity of our races, ethnicities, class backgrounds, of our herstories and our present lives.

We want to celebrate our BEING – our creativity, growth and risktaking – through sharings, exhibits of our artwork and crafts, music, readings, storytelling, dance and more.

Since the focus of the conference is the personal and political empowerment of old Lesbians, the program will center on small group discussions, not on keynote speakers.

Discussion groups include:

❖ *Lesbian Relationships in an Ageist Society*

❖ *Claiming Our Bodies / Ourselves*

❖ *Finding Community*

❖ *Ageism and Sexism in Lesbian / Gay Organizations*

❖ *Coming Out as an Old Lesbian*

❖ *Racism / Ableism / Classim*

❖ *Sharing Skills for Confronting Ageism and Lesbophobia*

Most discussion groups will be limited to Lesbians 60 and over. There will be ongoing groups for younger friends and partners to look at their relationships with older women in the past and present, and to find ways to work for change in their own lives and our communities.

- **ARTS**
  - **DANCE**
    - **CRAFTS**
      - **and MORE**

Why 60 and Over?

To avoid exploitation and to give old Lesbians the opportunity to be together without the oppression of younger Lesbians, we are LIMITING THE CONFERENCE TO LESBIANS 60 YEARS OF AGE AND OLDER. This age limit was imposed because old Lesbians are especially sensitive to those younger Lesbians and feminists who see themselves as committed to the old and tend to represent us, speak for us, and name us in ways that are self-serving, exploitive, and ageist.

In some ways, 60 might seem a very arbitrary age. It was chosen because the degree of oppression is greater beyond mid-life, after 60, when most of us know what it is to be perceived as "old".

In limiting attendance to Lesbians 60 and older, we do not want to imply that

being 60, 70, 80, or 90 are not distinct experiences, which we will be examining throughout the conference.

This is a conference by and for old Lesbians, 60 and over, both to celebrate and publicize our lives. There will be no keynote speakers. You are the star!

A Lesbian over 60 may invite ONE LESBIAN UNDER THE AGE OF 60 if she wishes to do so, keeping in mind the goals of the conference and the reasons for the age limitation.

If you are too young to attend, we're sorry. We hope you'll support us anyway, so that when you are sixty, ageism in our community, if not in society, will be much less.

Statetment of purpose from flyer announcing the First West Coast Old Lesbian Conference and Celebration. *Old Lesbians Organizing for Change Records*

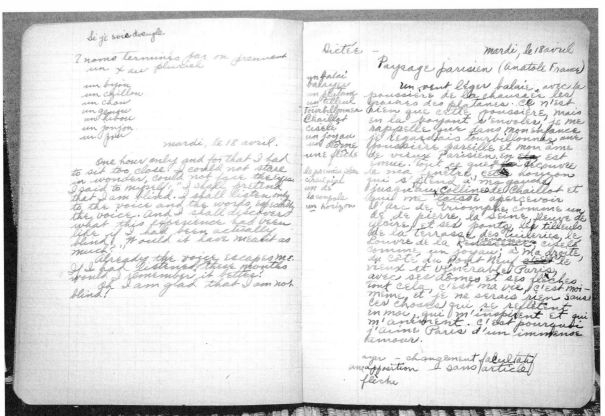

perspective of a man writing to his female muse, Alys. After receiving a B.A. in Journalism in 1934, Porter travelled out to California as a vagabond. She began to write about her experiences in personal diaries, a practice she maintained throughout her adult life.

In 1945 before the end of World War II, Porter joined the Women's Army Corps and served stateside for five years. During a trip to France in 1951, Porter discovered the poetry of Renée Vivien (1877–1909), and began using the name Gabrielle L'Autre to write lesbian poetry. Porter's time in France also inspired her to become an avid researcher and translator of Vivien's poetry, along with that of Natalie Clifford Barney (1976–1972) and other literary members of expatriate France.

Although the majority of Porter's written work remains unpublished, throughout the 1960s and 1970s she often contributed to small press publications including *The Archer, New Athenaeum, South and West, Tres Femme,* and *The Ladder.* During the same period of time Porter settled down in Oceanside, CA, and became active in lesbian and feminist groups. Porter served as editor for the local chapter of the Daughters of Bilitis, and later as co-founder of the groups Search and Tres Femme, for which she also wrote and edited newsletters and publications. In 1974, Porter published *White Heron: a collection of poems.* Along with Catherine Kroger, Porter was the first to publish English translations of Renée Vivien's poetry in the book, *Muse of the Violets* (1977). She died on May 30, 1989.

The collection contains drafts of her published and unpublished original poetry from 1928 to 1989, with the majority produced from the 1950s to the 1970s. Porter avidly researched and translated the work of Renée Vivien, Natalie Clifford Barney, and other women in their literary circle. The collection includes drafts of Porter's translations of French poetry, *White Heron: a collection of poems,* and *Muse of the Violets,* as well as photographs, correspondence, research files, materials related to her participation in lesbian and feminist organizations in the San Diego area, over six decades of personal diaries, and an extensive collection of rare books related to Porter's interests, including nineteenth- and twentieth-century French literature and poetry, lesbian history, feminism, and women in France.

Dianne Post Papers

COLLECTION ID: 2228
COLLECTION DATES: 1981–2003

Dianne Post is a lawyer who specializes in issues related to violence against women and children, including sex trafficking, pornography, and domestic violence. She has contributed to the design and implementation of legal policies and reform initiatives related to gender equality. She works with vulnerable populations in developing, transitional and developed countries. She consults on international cases, and has worked with the United Nations, the Inter-American Commission on Human Rights and the European Court of Human Rights. Collection contains materials related to lesbian and women's music and to the planning of the first women's music festival in Arizona.

Sue Prosin Papers

COLLECTION ID: 2225
COLLECTION DATES: 1960–1970

Sue Prosin was a social scientist and researcher, publishing studies on a range of topics throughout the 1960s and 1970s, including a comprehensive study on butch-femme lesbian relationships, which was published in 1962. She was also an active member of the Daughters of Bilitis. Collection contains research materials and the completed draft.

Corinna Radigan Papers

COLLECTION ID: 2193
COLLECTION DATES: 1960–1989

Corinna Radigan was a sports writer for several newspapers and magazines, including the *Bay Area Reporter*. This collection includes unpublished manuscripts and writings from Kary Wind, Lee Lynch, Shirley Gore, Rochelle Dubois and Corinna Radigan, as well as materials related to The Coming Out project, and correspondence between authors.

Ruth Reid and Kent Hyde Papers

COLLECTION ID: 1945
COLLECTION DATES: 1920–2001

Ruth Reid and Kent Hyde were both authors and lovers for over forty years. Their correspondence documents the changing political landscape of the twentieth century as well as their intellectual development and personal relationships. For most of their relationship, Kent Hyde, a woman, passed as a man.

Reid and Hyde lived in Berkeley, Santa Cruz, Fairfax, and Oakland, CA, and briefly in upstate New York. They had four years alone together before Kent's mother moved in with them, so that they could care for her. According to Reid, Kent's mother refused to acknowledge the couple's relationship during the fourteen years she lived with them.

They were not active participants in the gay movement. In fact, Reid has very few recollections of the time period related to gay activism or issues. Hyde identified as a communist for a brief time, and so followed activities of Joseph McCarthy and the House Un-American Activities Committee. Throughout the 1950s, Ruth and Kent owned and operated a weaving shop called Reid-Hyde Handweaving in San Francisco, doing both piecework and wholesale bulk items. Reid had learned weaving during her time in Germany and brought the skills to bear at a time when the two were out of work. Both wrote constantly. Hyde was a poet, published as early as the 1920s. Reid never finished her novel.

In her later years, Ruth became involved in the lesbian community. She worked on her writing in women's writing groups and developed supportive circles in the Berkeley area. Although her work was never published in its entirety, her autobiography, *Dark Birth*, was published in excerpts in *The Wild Iris*, *Gay Old Girls*, and *In the Life*. A version of *Dark Birth*, excerpted and with notes from Jacqueline Marie is

available under the title *Wife of a Lesbian*.

Drawing of Ruth Reid by Rudy Babcock.
Ruth Reid and Kent Hyde Papers

The collection includes the materials of Ruth Reid, Kent Hyde and Ruth "Rudy" Babcock, with whom Reid had an affair. Reid's materials include her unpublished manuscripts, letters, diary entries, and recordings of her reading and being interviewed. Hyde's materials include some published work, unpublished work, and letters. Babcock's materials include letters, drawings, and unpublished collaborative work with Reid. Also included is a taped interview from 1981 conducted by the archivists at the Mazer Archives. In it, Reid states that Hyde did not particularly like gays. She recalls two incidents in which Hyde's self-presentation drew attention to the couple, one in which they were confronted by the police and one in which their conservative neighbors had them under police surveillance. Much of the correspondence within the collection highlights their political beliefs and exchanges over a range of topics, but never explicitly addresses gay and lesbian issues. Their consistent and rich correspondence with friends and family document their lives in detail, including their tastes, opinions, beliefs, and relationships with others. Recordings of Hyde reading poetry can be found in the Mazer Collection of Audio Materials and Mazer Collection of Visual Materials.

Joan Robins Papers

COLLECTION ID: 1952
COLLECTION DATES: 1972–1985

Born in 1947, Joan Ellen Robins, also known as Joan Hoffman, was the co-founder, along with Dorothy Bricker and Marianne Yatrovsky, of the first consciousness-raising (CR) group in Los Angeles, CA. It convened at the Haymarket Center. Growing rapidly, the group was moved to a church in South Central Los Angeles that could accommodate its larger attendance. The group was notorious for dramatic and aesthetically detailed protesting tactics.

Robins also started the Women's Center in Los Angeles, which hosted various CR groups as well as labor union groups and lesbian activist groups. In 1968, Robins wrote the

Gay Pride flyer. *Joan Robins Papers*

Attendee at Gay Pride event. *Photo by Francesca Roccaforte. Francesca Roccaforte Papers*

Making Invisible Histories Visible

Handbook of Women's Liberation alongside her then-husband, Frank Hoffman. It was only available at the Women's Center. The group Lesbian Feminist, of which Robins was an original member, also originated at the Women's Center. The group staged protests interrupting the meetings of the National Organization for Women in order to bring lesbian visibility to the center of their agenda. Robins was also a founding member of the anti-rape squad in Los Angeles. In 1973, she helped to organize the Los Angeles Commission on Assaults Against Women. She became their director of education in 1975 and handled media appearances, commentary and out-reach programming. She eventually left the organization, as its rapid growth could not be supported by its infrastructure.

The collection contains documents relating to various lesbian and feminist organizations and conferences, including organizational documents, flyers, information pamphlets, newsletters, press releases, and handwritten notes. Also included is information related to organizing in defense of the Equal Rights Amendment, and reproductive rights and against the Family Protection Act.

Francesca Roccaforte Papers

COLLECTION ID: 2165
COLLECTION DATES: 1977–1994

Francesca Roccaforte is a photographer and teacher living in San Francisco, CA. She was born and raised in New York City, where her early love of photography and aesthetics was nurtured and developed by her parents and the environment.

Her first solo show was at an organization called "the Door" in the West Village in the 1970s. The Door nurtured her creative energy and enabled her to prepare for intense photographic studies at the School of Visual Arts and Creative Writing at Hunter College in New York. She spent four years immersed in photo studies, and working part time as a documentary photographer, performing arts photographer, and darkroom technician. She has taken workshops and classes with W. Eugene Smith, Ansel Adams, Eve Sonneman, Cora Wright Kennedy, Dena, and Alice Beck at the School of Visual Arts.

After a photography trip documenting spirituality and religious customs in Italy, Israel, and the United States, Roccaforte relocated to the San Francisco area at the age of 23. She was employed in several photography labs and camera stores and completed her visual arts education in California by earning degrees and/or certificates from the California College of Arts, Berkeley City College, and Cal State East Bay. Her thesis project, which focused on portraits and accompanying oral herstories of Italian women, was exhibited and published in the 1990s.

Roccaforte has worked as a freelance photographer, been employed in educational and medical institutions, and assisted with production and operational aspects of film festivals. Currently, she teaches beginning and advanced digital photography to adult learners. She also exhibits her photographic art in the Bay Area.

Photos by Francesca Roccaforte. Francesca Roccaforte Papers

HER NAVAJO RELATIVES ACCUSE HER OF "PASSING FOR WHITE"

Artwork by Tyger-Womon. *Tyger-Womon Papers*

This collection consists primarily of photographs taken by Roccaforte. The photographs that make up the collection are assembled from different series and focus on disparate subjects, including gay and lesbian pride events, horse racing, cultural events, and self-portraits. Also included in the collection are poems written by Roccaforte, as well as documents related to her professional and academic achievement.

Judith Saunders Papers

COLLECTION ID: 2221
COLLECTION DATES: 1971–1976

Judith Saunders was a registered nurse and advocate for gay and lesbian rights. Throughout her career she published works on topics relating to the affective relationship between nurses and their patients, specific needs and risks of working with gay and lesbian populations, and heterosexism in the medical profession. She was the associate editor of *Before Stonewall: Activists for Gay and Lesbian Rights in Historical Context*. The collection includes correspondence, newsletters and pamphlets from LGBT organizations, correspondence, notes, samples, and examples from Maud Gonne Press.

Ardy Tibby Papers

COLLECTION ID: 2167
COLLECTION DATES: 1941–1989

Born in 1941, Ardy Tibby became a teacher in the late 1960s. After coming out as a lesbian, Ardy Tibby joined the lesbian activist and cultural community. She began performing as a

storyteller in festivals and community events, touring with artists such as Chocolate Waters throughout the 1980s and participating in the Califia community. She was a co-founder of the lesbian production group Delta Pi in 1984, which operated in Santa Rosa, CA, until 1989. She was the guest editor of a special issue, titled "Willing Up and Keeling Over: a Lesbian Handbook of Death Rights and Rituals," of *Sinister Wisdom 80*. She has been and is currently involved with Older Lesbians Organizing for Change, the Lesbian Archives, and the Women's Circus. She resides with her partner Jean Taylor in Victoria, Australia. She refers to herself as a "proud, loud, bearded lesbian."

The bulk of the collection represents 1970 to 1985, when she was involved in lesbian community organizations as an organizer, storyteller, and participant in California and Phoenix, AZ. A large part of the collections is made up of photographs, journals, and scrapbook pages covering her early life. Also included is correspondence between Tibby and various friends and colleagues. Although parts of the collection deal with tour logistics, the majority of its materials are personal and community oriented.

Kitty Tsui Papers

COLLECTION ID: 1949
COLLECTION DATES: 1977–1993

Although born in Hong Kong in 1952, Kitty Tsui spent her childhood in California and earned a degree in creative writing from San Francisco State University. Her poetry and prose have been published in over thirty-five anthologies, including *Chloe Plus Olivie* (1994) and *Lesbian Erotics* (1995). In 1995, she received the Center for Lesbian and Gay Studies Ken Sawson Award for research in gay and lesbian history, and was also listed as one of the fifty most influential people in gay and lesbian literature by Lambda Book Report. She has been featured in three films, *Women of Gold* (1990), *Framing Lesbian Fashion* (1992), and *Cut Sleeve* (1992). Tsui is the author of three books: *The Words of a Woman who Breathes Fire, Breathless,* and *Sparks Fly. Breathless* won the Firecracker Alternative Book Award from the American Booksellers Association in 1996. Her third book, *Sparks Fly,* was penned by her alter ego, Eric Norton, a gay leatherman in pre-AIDS San Francisco. Tsui is also a competitive bodybuilder. She earned a bronze medal at the Gay Games in San Francisco in 1986 and a gold medal in Vancouver in 1990. This collection includes Tsui's prose writings, correspondence, clippings, reviews, and poetry.

Tyger-Womon Papers

COLLECTION ID: 1943
COLLECTION DATES: 1992–1994

Tyger-Womon was a writer, artist, and Native American shaman. Also known as V.L. Adams, very little information can be found on Tyger-Womon before or after the two-year period reflected in this collection. The collection includes materials related to photography projects, interviews, poetry,

ASIAN/PACIFIC LESBIANS
OUR IDENTITIES, OUR MOVEMENTS

SUNDAY, SEPTEMBER 27

6:00 Refreshments
7:00 Program
8:30 Reception

MISSION CULTURAL CENTER
2868 Mission Street (at 25th)
San Francisco

$5 Donation (toward program
tour to NY-DC-Chicago)
For information: 626-6441

POETRY, DRAMATIC READING
By Kitty Tsui

"COMING OUT, COMING TOGETHER"
By Trinity Ordoña
A slideshow on Asian/Pacific
lesbians featured at recent
Lesbians of Color Conference

SPEECH
By Virginia Benavidez
National March on Washington for
Lesbian and Gay Rights

Sponsored by Kitty Tsui/Trinity Ordoña in conjunction with
The National March on Washington for Lesbian and Gay Rights

Flyer for "Asian/Pacific Lesbians: Our Identities, Our Movements." *Kitty Tsui Papers*

The Woman's Building and
Sensor: Women's Media Resource Center Present:

WOMEN ARTIST FILMMAKERS

Two Evenings with Alida Walsh at the Woman's Building,
1727 N. Spring Street,
(just south of Chinatown)
Los Angeles, CA 90012
tel. 221-6161

Fri July 14 **8pm**
Films from Women/ Artist/ Filmmakers of New York

Sat July 15 8pm
Films and Multi-media by Alida Walsh

Alida Walsh will be present both evenings for discussion

$2.50 for Woman's Building & Sensor Members
$3.00 non-members

Also:

A Seminar with Alida Walsh
Sat July 22 – 1 pm
Upstairs at Fox Venice Theater
620 Lincoln Blvd., Venice

Alida will discuss her film techniques in relation
to her art, – and show a ½" videotape she produced.
Open discussion follows.

$3.00 for Woman's Building & Sensor Members
$5.00 non-members

songs, and writings spanning 1992 to 1994. All contents are her work, with the exception of collaborative projects with Hanh Thi Pham, a Vietnamese-American artist. Also included are three audiotapes of exchanges between Tyger-Womon and Hanh Thi Pham.

Carol Waymire Collection

COLLECTION ID: 2172
COLLECTION DATES: 1910–1993

Carol Marie Waymire is a California-based lawyer who serves underrepresented communities through her work on immigration law, rights of undocumented workers, racial and sexual discrimination, worker rights, and child custody for gay parents. Born in 1933, she graduated from Santa Rosa High School in Sonoma County, CA. Waymire was the first of her family to go to college, graduating from San Jose State University in 1956 with a major in Social Sciences and a minor in English.

She taught junior high school for a number of years before joining the newly formed Peace Corps and traveling to Ghana for two years to teach English at a government school for girls. While she later questioned the motivations and consequences of the organization's work abroad, the experience

This flyer for a filmmaking workshop at the Woman's Building exemplifies their commitment to support working artists and to mentor new ones. *Woman's Building Records*

shaped her path. She earned a Master's in teaching English as a Second Language at UCLA in 1966, after which she taught ESL for more than ten years in Los Angeles at the Evans Adult School.

Her experience teaching non-English speaking adults, largely people from Asia and Latin America who faced poverty and racial and class discrimination yet had no resources or recourse to legal support, drew Waymire to pursue law. She received her law degree from The People's College of Law (1977–1981), a private, nonprofit law school in downtown Los Angeles which offers an evening program aimed at progressive social change and social justice.

Active in lesbian, gay and feminist activism in Los Angeles, and California more broadly, Waymire was involved in organizations and causes such as the LA Women's Forum, Lesbian Feminists of LA, and the movement against Proposition 6 in 1978. More generally, she was active on issues such as gay rights, violence against women, and abortion.

This collection contains periodicals, ephemera, and informational literature related to her lesbian, gay, feminist, and socialist interests. The periodicals, which make up the bulk

Making Invisible Histories Visible

of the collection, cover a wide range of cultural, political and economic issues related to gay rights and women's rights. These include LA-based publications, as well as those from California and the rest of the country.

Carolyn Weathers Papers

COLLECTION ID: 2223
COLLECTION DATES: 1980–1989

Carolyn Weathers (*shown at left in photo*) is a lesbian activist and publisher. Born in 1941, Carolyn Weathers was the daughter of a Southern Baptist preacher. She moved to Los Angeles after being expelled from a university in Texas when she came out as a lesbian. She was an enthusiastic participant in the pre-Stonewall bar scene of San Antonio, TX. She was a participant in the Gay Liberation Front and in the Gay Women's Liberation Front at the Women's Center of Los Angeles. In 1986, Weathers and artist Jenny Wrenn founded Clothespin Fever Press, a lesbian book publishing company which operated until 1994. Weathers' stories and remembrances are included in *Gay L.A.: A History of Sexual Outlaws, Power Politics, and Lipstick Lesbians* and *Feminists Who Changed America 1963–1975*. After retiring as a public librarian for the Los Angeles Public Library, she began writing the column "True Life Lesbian Adventures" for the newsletter of June L. Mazer Lesbian Archives.

This collection contains materials from the founding and operation of Clothespin Fever Press. In particular, it contains correspondence, memos, handwritten notes, diaries, programs, reports, and film leading up to, documenting the production of, and resulting from the Farmersville Film Project. The materials, many created by Henry Lanford, were gathered by Baylis Glascock, a cinematographer on the Farmersville Film Project.

Woman's Building Records

COLLECTION ID: 1982
COLLECTION DATES: 1975–1994

The Woman's Building was a nonprofit arts and education center located in Los Angeles, CA. It focused on feminist art and served as a venue for the women's movement. The Woman's Building began as the Feminist Studio Workshop (FSW), founded in 1973 by art critic and historian Arlene Raven, designer Sheila Levant de Bretteville, and artist Judy Chicago. It was one of the first schools for women artists. At the core of the FSW's mission was the centrality of art practice to the larger women's movement.

A rented space in downtown Los Angeles became the home of the FSW and was eventually named the Woman's

Celestial goddesses of Cambodia who personify the moist vapours of mists and clouds. Their posture of flight is enacted in modern Cambodian dance.

"Aspara" postcard from the Woman's Building's "The Postcard Project: Celebrating Our Heroines," a project organized by Cheri Gaulke. More than three hundred cards were created by a range of women and featured mothers, poets, goddesses, workers, writers, and artists. Heroines included poets Edna St. Vincent Millay and Rabia of Basra, artist Rosa Bonheur, writer Zora Neale Hurston, quilter and historian Phyllis Carter, sculptor Nancy Graves and the Sleeping Lady of Saflieni sculpture. *Woman's Building Records*

Building (the name was taken from the structure created for the World's Columbian Exposition in Chicago in 1893). The Woman's Building was a shared space for the FSW, Womanspace Gallery, the Women's Liberation Union, and the National Organization of Women.

In 1975 the FSW moved to a new space, and by 1977 most of the other organizations had departed. The FSW voted to hire administrative staff and implement a board structure in order to solidify responsibility for the building and all other legal and financial concerns. The funding for the building would then come from membership, fund raising, grant money, tuition from workshops and courses, and the board members themselves. FSW officially closed in 1981, but the Woman's Building continued to provide educational resources. The main focus transitioned to artistic programming, including visual art, performance art, readings, and video art.

Summer 1983

The Woman's Building 1973-1983 — celebrating our tenth anniversary as a public center for women's culture.

NEA Grant for Artists' Books, Postcards

The Women's Graphic Center is proud to announce that we have received our second $25,000 Artists Organizations Grant from the National Endowment for the Arts. As with last year's grant, $10,000 of these funds will go directly to artists, who will be commissioned by the WGC to produce work. $6,000 is allocated to artists to produce artists' books, and $4,000 will be awarded to artists to make postcards.

Beginning in the fall of 1983, the Women's Graphic Center will send out a call for entries to women artists who wish to apply in either of these categories. A panel of judges will select from these entries the artists who will receive honoraria to produce books and postcards.

Entries will not be accepted before September 15, 1983. If you wish to receive information about the competition, send an S.A.S.E. to Susan King, at the Women's Graphic Center.

Jill Littlewood:
A Book Show
A Drawing Show

"Collages came first, and then drawings. Now they both get made into books," says Jill Littlewood of her work for the show opening June 4 at the gallery of the Woman's Building.

The drawings will include scientific illustrations currently being made for National Geographic Foundation, and science fiction/fantasy illustrations for books published both privately and for Ballantine – DelRey books. Collages and their evolution into sequential one-of-a-kind books will also be shown.

The show will run June 4 – 25. The opening reception for for the artist is June 4 from 3 – 6 p.m.

Woman's Building Will Stay on Spring Street

In last-minute negotiations with the landlord, the Woman's Building has renewed its lease on the building which it has occupied since 1975, at 1727 North Spring Street. While the decision does mean an increase in rent, it also represents substantial savings in moving costs.

Administrative Director Sue Maberry explains, "The MOVE Committee of the Board investigated a number of different sites, everything from a warehouse in downtown L.A. to a mansion in Hollywood to the Old Venice Jail. Several options had very attractive aspects, but none were as financially feasible as staying on North Spring. This way we'll be putting money into upgrading our facility – making it wheelchair accessible, developing a conference room/ meeting space, enlarging our gallery, etc."

The Board of Directors has outlined a plan to accomplish major renovations by the end of 1983. We will be seeking volunteers to help with painting, moving, building, and other activities.

In November of this year, we will be celebrating our 10th Anniversary as a public center for women's culture with exhibitions, performances, our Second Annual Vesta Awards, and other exciting public events.

Welcome Aboard!

We'd like to welcome the following women who have joined our Board of Directors this year: Annette Colfax (financial manager); Ena Dubnoff (architect); Vicki Madrid (photographer); Shirley Pettaway-Blue (financial consultant); Hye Sook (painter); Sharon Spencer (artist); Christine Tripp (fundraiser); and Mitsuye Yamada (writer). We're very excited and pleased to have their involvement in the Woman's Building.

Summer 1983 issue of the Women's Graphic Center newsletter. *Woman's Building Records*

Making Invisible Histories Visible

Sunday	Monday	Tuesday	Wednesday	Thursday	Friday	Saturday
Sept.		**1** *Exhibit:* The Quest For Balance continues thru Sept. 25 *Exhibit:* Celebrating our Heroines: The Postcard Project exhibition continues thru Sept. 25	**2**	**3** *Geraldine Hanon's postcard celebrates the creators of Astrology* ▼	**4** *Fringe Festival Workshop:* Stamp Happy, 11 a.m. – 1 p.m. *Cable Show:* Putting Our Hands to Other Labor, 8 p.m. on United, and 9:30 p.m. on Valley	**5** *Holiday:* The Woman's Building will be closed
6 *Cable Show:* Putting Our Hands to Other Labor, 9:30 p.m. on Communicom	**7** *Holiday:* The Woman's Building will be closed	**8** *New Limited Edition Artists' Postcards on sale through September 25*			**11** *Exhibit:* The Quest For Balance continues thru Sept. 25, a Fringe Festival Event *Cable Show:* Putting Our Hands to Other Labor, 8 p.m. on United	**12** *Class:* Women's Video Access, 10 a.m. – 1 p.m. *New Limited Edition Artists' Postcards on sale through September 25*
13 Go Shining!		**15** ◄ *Postcard tribute to Medicine Woman Evelyn Eaton by Joan Robins*	**16**	**17** *New Limited Edition Artists' Postcards on sale through September 25*	**18** *Exhibit:* The Quest For Balance, a Fringe Festival Event	**19** *Workshop:* Gift Of The Twisted Hair, 11 a.m. – 4 p.m. *Class:* Women's Video Access, 10 a.m. – 1 p.m.
20	**22**	**23**	**24** ◄ *Sonia Johnson postcard by D. Jesse Stumpp*		**25** *Last day to view exhibits:* The Quest For Balance and The Postcard Project: Celebrating Our Heroines	**26** *"Man and Mountain 11" by Lita Albuquerque, part of Earth Vision / Human Scale* ▼
27	**28**	**29** DIRECT DIAL HEROINES WOMEN'S 87 ◄ *Tecaral Haggerty celebrates the Women's Yellow Pages in this postcard*				

Events calendar, September, 1987. *Woman's Building Records*

In 1981, the Women's Graphic Center (WGC) Typesetting and Design was created as the profit-making operation. WGC provided typesetting, printing, and design and production services. Its profits supported the other activities of the Woman's Building. That year, the Woman's Building also began renting studio space in order to generate additional revenue. WGC closed in 1988. The Woman's Building closed later in 1991. This collection shows the myriad functions of the Woman's Building, and its central place in the feminist movement as a hub of the creation and display of feminist art and a community educational facility throughout its eighteen-year history.

The Woman's Building collective produced and distributed newsletters to their supporters and members on a monthly basis that included announcements, developments, solicitations for donations, and event calendars. Included in this collection are newsletters documenting the activities, publications, and outreach efforts of the WGC from 1983 to 1990. In addition, there are several publications from the WGC, including products of a letterpress workshop as well as one of their artist publications.

Produced in the WGC–but not as a part of the for-profit operation–was the collaborative Postcard Project led by artist-in-residence Cheri Gaulke. The project ran from 1985 to 1988, generating hundreds of limited-edition postcards, many of which are included here.

Also included are descriptive press materials from the LA Women's Video Center (LAWVC), which was founded in 1976 and provided classes, equipment, and support to women interested in using video to produce documentation, public service announcements, center productions, and art tapes.

The Women's Press Collective was founded in 1969 by artists Wendy Cadden and Judy Grahn. Dedicated to publishing the "work of women that we thought no one else would do," the selections in this collection display particular activist works surrounding individual women including Joan Little and Inez García.

A large element of the collection consists of the exhibition catalogs, with many containing essays or other writings by Arlene Raven. The collection also includes press releases from the Woman's Building about performances, community events, lectures and workshops, as well as articles and clippings from outside news sources concerning activities at the Woman's Building.

Boxes of materials at the June L. Mazer Lesbian Archives in West Hollywood, CA. *Photo by Angela Brinskele.*
Angela Brinskele Papers

Appendix A

'ACCESS MAZER' PROJECT: ORGANIZING AND
DIGITIZING THE LESBIAN-FEMINIST ARCHIVE IN LOS ANGELES

CSW'S INITIAL ENGAGEMENT with the June L. Mazer Lesbian Archives was a project titled "Access Mazer: Organizing and Digitizing the Lesbian-Feminist Archive in Los Angeles." As part of CSW's large-scale research project on "A History of Women's Social Movement Activities in Los Angeles, 1960–1999," CSW worked with the Mazer Archives to inventory, organize, preserve, and digitize five key Los Angeles-themed collections. The project was partially supported by the UCLA Center for Community Partnerships. The digitized materials and finding aids are available at the UCLA Library website. The finding aids are also available from the Online Archive of California.

A symposium, "Processing the Lesbian Archive: The 'Access Mazer' Project," was held on May 5, 2009, to commemorate the completion of the two-year project. Speakers included Ann Cvetkovich, professor at the University of Texas at Austin and author of *An Archive of Feelings: Trauma, Sexuality, and Lesbian Public Cultures,* as well as James Hixon, Candace Moore, and T-Kay Sangwand, who were all graduate students who worked on the processing of the collections. Videocasts are available for viewing.

This project—and the partnership between CSW, the Mazer Archives, and the UCLA Library that formed from it—ultimately led to "Making Invisible Histories Visible," the project celebrated in this book.

Connexxus/Centro de Mujeres Collection

COLLECTION ID: 1848
COLLECTION DATES: 1985–1991

In early 1984, Adel Martinez and Lauren Jardine conceived the idea behind Connexxus, a women-run center in Los Angeles that would provide quality and comprehensive services that catered to women, particularly lesbians. In May of 1984, a group of women met to discuss how to bring it into fruition. They envisioned a space in which lesbians could thrive professionally, personally, and socially. In January 1985, Connexxus opened its doors on Santa Monica Boulevard in West Hollywood. Connexxus' initial space was a 1400-square-foot facility with ten rooms that served as space for a library, workshops, rap groups, counseling, meetings, and other social activities. Lauren Jardine, Ph.D., was hired as the Executive Director. Connexxus operated for six years out of West Hollywood. In 1986, it opened Connexxus East/ Centro de Mujeres, a satellite location in East Los Angeles. Connexxus offered a variety of services at its two locations, including referrals, support groups, counseling/ therapy services, workshops, social events, and a coffeehouse. Connexxus East specifically did outreach to Latina lesbians in East L.A.

When Connexxus opened, it filled the vacuum for a public space for women/lesbians in Los Angeles. During its operation, other specialized organizations and businesses emerged to serve the dynamic lesbian population in the city, which was reflected in a decline in users of the Connexxus programs. Collection contains administrative records.

Margaret Cruikshank Collection

COLLECTION ID: 1847
COLLECTION DATES: 1971–1986

A native of northern Minnesota, Margaret (Peg) Cruikshank came out as a lesbian in the 1960s. With a Ph.D. in Victorian literature from Loyola University in Chicago, IL, Cruikshank began teaching English in 1969 at various colleges and universities in the Midwest. In 1975, she began teaching at Mankato State University (now called Minnesota State

University, Mankato), which did not have a women's studies program. She helped establish the first women's studies department and served as director from 1975 to 1977. Her experience as a closeted academic then as an open lesbian in a university setting started her on a path to a lifelong commitment to increasing the visibility and solidarity of lesbians within the academic profession.

She lived in the Midwest until 1977, when she moved to San Francisco, where she played an active role in the efflorescence of lesbian feminist politics and culture at the time. Writing under her own name as well as various pseudonyms, Cruikshank wrote numerous essays, articles, and reviews for such periodicals as *Gay Community News, Motheroot Journal, The Radical Teacher, Focus, Journal of Homosexuality,* and *The Advocate.*

In August 1980, she became head of a small program in Continuing Education at the University of San Francisco (USF) but was fired after five months. Subsequently, Cruikshank taught at City College of San Francisco (CCSF) and worked with other faculty and administrators to incorporate lesbian and gay studies into the curriculum. These efforts resulted in the organization of the Castro/Valencia Campus and the appointment of Cruikshank as the first woman to teach a gay and lesbian literature course. She taught an introductory women's studies course and lesbian and gay literature and later courses on aging and women. Cruikshank has edited three major anthologies on lesbians: *The Lesbian Path, Lesbian Studies,* a women's history/lesbian studies text, and *New Lesbian Writing,* a lesbian literature anthology. Her most recent anthology, *Fierce with Reality: an Anthology of Literature about Aging,* grew out of her thesis for a Master's degree in gerontology at San Francisco State University. Her other books include *Thomas Babington Macaulay, The Gay and Lesbian Liberation Movement,* and *Learning to be Old: Gender, Culture, and Aging.*

The collection holds a mixture of professional and personal papers, including materials related to the writing of her first three anthologies, as well as her correspondence and other publications. Her correspondence also traces the networks of lesbian critics, academics, and writers that were established through panels at the Modern Language Association's and Gay Academic Union's annual conventions, pioneering lesbian feminist periodicals of the 1970s, lesbian groups, women's studies programs, writing workshops, and women's publishing presses.

Lillian Faderman Collection

COLLECTION ID: 1849
COLLECTION DATES: 1976–1989

Lillian Faderman is an internationally known literary scholar and historian of lesbian history. She has published nine books and numerous articles on lesbian history, literature and criticism, including *Surpassing the Love of Men,* an acclaimed study of five centuries of love between women, and *Odd Girls and Twilight Lovers,* a history of twentieth-century

lesbians in America. Both were named among *The New York Times* notable books of the year. Most recently, she has published a memoir, *Naked in the Promised Land,* and *Gay L.A.,* which she co-authored with Stuart Timmons, and *My Mother's Wars.*

Faderman's work has centered on establishing a lesbian tradition, on what she calls a "usable past." In her early works, she showed that so-called romantic friendships between women were considered neither abnormal nor undesirable in prior centuries. Accordingly, women who loved women in the past were not always made to live like outlaws. Faderman has also written on the theme of same-sex love and romantic friendship in the poems and letters of Emily Dickinson; in novels by Henry James, Oliver Wendell Holmes, and Henry Wadsworth Longfellow; and in popular magazine fiction of the early twentieth century.

Faderman's later book, *To Believe in Woman: What Lesbians Have Done for America–A History* is the culmination of her two previous works. It charts romantic friendships between women and lesbian love through some of the most important social movements in the U.S. and shows how these same-sex partnerships made major feminist causes of the nineteenth and early twentieth centuries possible.

Throughout her career, Faderman has been sought after as a speaker, teacher, critic, and visiting lecturer. She has been a frequent speaker at lesbian and feminist organizations, universities, and lesbian, gay and women's organizations nationally and internationally, including the Modern Language Association, the National Women's Studies Association, Gay Academic Union, and the Berkshire Women's History Conference.

The collection includes materials from her professional life. Among the papers are drafts of a published papers, book reviews, and manuscript drafts for three of her books, correspondence, publicity materials, background research, contracts and royalty statements, printed matter, photographs, and audio materials.

Southern California Women for Understanding Collection

COLLECTION ID: 1851
COLLECTION DATES: 1975–1999

Southern California Women for Understanding (SCWU), an educational nonprofit organization, was formed in 1976 to enhance "the quality of life for [the lesbian] community and for lesbians nationwide, creative and positive exchange about homosexuality, [and to change] stereotypical images of lesbians." At its height, SCWU reached membership of 1,100. In 1982, *Lesbian News* hailed it as the "largest lesbian support group in the country."

SCWU originated as a support group of the Whitman-Radclyffe Foundation, a San Francisco–based gay rights organization that strove to educate the public on homosexuality. In 1976, Betty Berzon, one of the foundation's few female board members, invited twenty women to form the Southern California Women for Whitman-Radclyffe Foundation. After forming a steering committee and electing officers, the women planned a series of "Special Interest Raps" which would allow lesbian women to come together and informally discuss a variety of topics. Founder Betty Berzon, a licensed psychotherapist who was one of the first to work with gay and lesbian clients, led SCWU's first Special Interest Rap, "Disclosing Your Gayness to Family and Friends."

After it and WRF mutually severed ties, SCWU focused efforts on educational and social events programming, fundraising, legislative lobbying, and fostering projects for the lesbian community (for example, Connexxus/Centro de Mujeres). In addition to its grassroots efforts in building a social space for the lesbian community in Los Angeles, SCWU strove to work with high-profile figures. Its annual Lesbian Rights Award Dinner would honor a lesbian woman whose work benefited lesbians on a large scale. Honorees include Del Martin and Phyllis Lyon (founders of Daughters of Bilitis), Elsa Gidlow (poet), Dianne Abbit and Roberta Bennett (attorneys, founders of first Sexuality and Lesbian Task Forces of the National Organization of Women's Los Angeles chapter), Virginia Uribe (founder of Project 10), Adrienne Rich (writer), Gloria E. Anzaldúa (writer), Cherríe Moraga (writer), and Jackie Goldberg (member of the Los Angeles City Council).

As an educational organization, SCWU hosted a variety of educational programs, including informal rap groups, theater productions (*Welcome to Our Lesbian World*), and guest speakers. Additionally, SCWU's research committee designed and executed studies on lesbian lifestyles in Los Angeles. In 1977, SCWU surveyed its membership, asking questions about family, religion, education, work, health, and experiences with social and employment discrimination. They received 1,000 responses and the results were published in the SCWU newsletter. In addition to the projects planned and executed by the central organization, SCWU had numerous area chapters that would plan and execute their own projects and events tailored to their respective constituencies. SCWU's membership consisted primarily of professional, middle and upper-class women, the majority of whom were white. In response to accusations of elitism, the Board of Directors began an internal dialogue on diversity in 1989. The collection contains the operational records.

Women Against Violence Against Women Collection

COLLECTION ID: 1850
COLLECTION DATES: 1964–1994

Women Against Violence Against Women (WAVAW) formed out of an ad-hoc coalition of feminist groups who joined forces to protest a film called *Snuff* and the advertising campaign for the Rolling Stones album, *Black and Blue.* Advertised as having been made in South America where

"life is cheap" and claiming to show the actual murder and dismemberment of a woman, *Snuff* debuted in March of 1976 in twenty-two theaters in Los Angeles and Orange County. Because of WAVAW protests, film was withdrawn from circulation in the entire Southern California area one week after it opened.

In June of 1976, a billboard on Hollywood's Sunset Strip, advertised the Rolling Stones' album *Black and Blue,* which was released on Atlantic Records, a subsidiary of Warner Communications, Inc. It depicted a beaten, bound woman saying, "I'm 'Black and Blue' from the Rolling Stones and I love it!" The sign was removed during the night before a press conference that WAWAV had scheduled at the site.

In response to pressure from WAVAW, Atlantic Records scaled back its advertising campaign for the record but did not eliminate it. WAVAW responded by starting a campaign to stop the use of images of violence against women in advertising. When Warner, Elektra, and Atlantic Records—all subsidiaries of Warner Communications, Inc. (WCI)—failed to respond, WAVAW, in combination with the California state chapter of the National Coalition for Women, called for a boycott in December of 1976. Thousands of letters demanded that the companies institute a responsible advertising policy. The letter-writing campaign developed as a follow-up to a slideshow created by WAVAW, a presentation of offensive album covers that was shown at women's groups, schools, universities, and organizations across the country.

In 1979, after three years of national protests, community slide shows, letter writing, phone calling, protests as shareholders' meetings, leafletting, and boycotting, WAVAW secured a policy from Warner Communications, Inc., which stated that they had agreed to cease and desist in the use of images of violence against women as an advertising gimmick. On November 8, 1979, WAVAW and WCI announced that an agreement had been reached at press conferences in New York and Los Angeles. The agreement was presented to the public in the form of a joint press statement, which was negotiated by representatives from WAVAW's national coordinating committee and from the office of David H. Horowitz, who was in charge of WCI's record division.

Subsequently, the Los Angeles chapter of WAVAW turned to local projects, protesting against a United Artists film *Windows* in November/December 1980 and against *Playboy*'s First Amendment Awards in 1982.

The collection contains a mixture of papers and organizational records, publications, ephemera and audiovisual materials collected by organization member Dani Adams. Of particular interest are the internal memos and a complete run of national newsletters produced by the Los Angeles chapter for national distribution, as well as slides and scripts from the WAVAW slideshow.

Building in West Hollywood, CA, where The June L. Mazer Lesbian Archives is located.
Photo by Angela Brinskele. Angela Brinskele Papers

Appendix B
DONATING TO THE JUNE L. MAZER LESBIAN ARCHIVES

THE JUNE L. MAZER LESBIAN ARCHIVES has resided in the Wherle Building in West Hollywood since the late 1980s. The Mazer Archives has been supported by private donors, several foundations, volunteers, and the City of West Hollywood.

INSIDE THE WALLS OF THE MAZER
As you walk inside the doors of the Mazer, you are immersed in women's history—more than a hundred years of it. We have feminist and lesbian memorabilia of all kinds, as well as women's manuscripts, journals, books and published periodicals. Included are personal letters and scrapbooks, private letters, artwork, music and audio recordings, newspapers, buttons, photographs, videos, flyers, magazines and papers from lesbian organizations, and even clothing, such as softball team uniforms from the 1940s and 1950s and World War II uniforms. There are many ways to get involved:

- Give financially
- Volunteer
- Diversify our collection
- Share our work
- Join our oral history project
- Create a box of your life

HELPING WOMEN LIVE FOREVER
The Mazer's work is mainly supported by donations from incredibly generous women (and a few men!) across the world. You can give a one-time or monthly gift for a specific project, or support all of our archival and outreach work through our general operating budget.

MAZER'S ORAL HISTORY PROJECT
Let us know if you are interested in doing an oral history with us.

THE BOX PROJECT
The Mazer's Box Project was created by Angela Brinskele and Dr. Marie Cartier. It was born out of the pain of lost lesbian lives and their collections. Unfortunately, women often die without preparing something that informs people of their wishes. We have often heard about and seen family members visiting someone's home after she dies and tossing everything she owned into a dumpster. Whether they do this due to estrangement, homophobia or because they didn't know her wishes—the artifacts of her life are still gone.

Anyone who would like to donate a collection can get a box from the Archives and take it home and fill it up in her own time. The box is well labeled and has a deed inside so that if the owner dies before donating, it the box will provide a "path of clear intention."

By creating a safe place for lesbian and feminist history, we are paving the way for future generations to understand more fully their own identity and history and help maintain this vital link. Your passion and commitment can help ensure that we can continue to reach thousands of people each year and inspire each woman to live more fully by knowing–and sharing—her own history. You can help women live forever–at the Mazer Archives. Together, we help protect, share and make accessible our collective history now and for generations to come.

VISITING
If you have a research project or just have a passion to explore feminist and lesbian history, call to set up an appointment. We're also open most first Sundays of the month and every Tuesday, from 11 to 3. Call or email or check the website for details.

JUNE L. MAZER LESBIAN ARCHIVES
626 N. Robertson Blvd./P.O. Box 691866

West Hollywood, CA 90069

(310) 659-2478

EMAIL: contact@mazerlesbianarchives.org

WEBSITE: www.mazerlesbianarchives.org

BLOG: mazerlesbianarchives.blog spot.com

Chronology

by BEN RAPHAEL SHER

1981 The West Coast Lesbian Collections, now called The June L. Mazer Archives, then called is founded in Oakland, CA.

1981 Ruth Reid donates the collection of her and her partner Kent Hyde (who died in 1968) to the West Coast Lesbian Collections.

1982 First issue of *In the Life* newsletter published.

1982 The Great American Lesbian Art Show, 1980, collection donated.

1982 Jean (Lewis) Miller, 1929–1980, collection donated

1982 Records of Diana Press, Inc., donated.

1982 Marion Zimmer Bradley collection donated

1983 Anne D'Arcy, Bunny MacCulloch, and Evan Rubin donate to the periodical collection.

1983 Grant from Golden Gate Business Association funds membership campaign.

1987 Archives move to Los Angeles.

1987 June L. Mazer dies

1987 After June L. Mazer dies, the Archives acquires its present name in honor of her work as a community activist and her invaluable support.

1989 Archives earn 501(C)(3) nonprofit status and receive donated space from the City of West Hollywood, where it continues to reside.

1991 First issue *In the Life* newsletter published since the name change. Lillian Faderman and Marie Cartier donate materials.

1992 Judy Freespirit donates materials.

1993 President of the Board Claudia Brink and Secretary of the Board Carol Fulton resign upon completing their terms.

1993 Lillian Faderman, Alice Hom, Lourdes Arguelles, Alycee Lane, and Kim Kralj join the Board of the Mazer.

1993 First benefit at Pacific Design Center (September 26)

1995 Ivy Bottini and Jeanne Cordova join of the Board of the Mazer.

1995 Archives acquire the records of *Broomstick Magazine.*

1996 The Archives' space undergoes its first renovation

1996 Ann L. Giagni becomes President of the Board of Mazer.
Terri de la Peña donates her papers.

1996 Judith Twentyman and Diana Griffiths join the Board of the Mazer.

1996 First website, www.lesbian.org/mazer, debuts and efforts to create a computerized catalog of their holdings are begun.

1996 Website receives a Rainbow Award for its contribution to the LGBT community. The award is given for "excellence in content, design, creativity, presentation, or overall concept" of a home web page.

1997 Margaret (Peg) Cruikshank donates her papers.

1997 First Dyke-Utante Ball held.

1997 Myra Ridell joins the Board of the Mazer.

1998 Diane Germain donates papers and Dr. William Moritz donates Margaret A. Porter Papers.

1998 Mazer receives L. Dianne Anderson Trust Funds.

1998 The Mazer's space in West Hollywood undergoes a major renovation.

1998: Christine Jehanne Burton dies, bequeathing her library of books to The Mazer Collection.

1999 Judy Tupac, DDS, dies, bequeathing her papers.

2000 The June L. Mazer Collection changes its name to The June L. Mazer Lesbian Archives

2000 Mazer receives first of many grants from the Liberty Hill Foundation. Grants supports the ongoing cataloging project.

2000 Oral history project begins to document lesbian feminist community.

2000 Susan Brilliant dies, bequeathing her collection and naming the Mazer as a beneficiary in her will.

2001 The Mazer receives the first of several grants from the Durfee Foundation to help with getting their catalog on the Internet.

2001 Pat Nordell donates her collection of papers, much of it dealing with her life in sports.

2001 Running out of space, Mazer begins to seek donation of new space.

2004 New website, mazerlesbianarchives.org, is launched, allowing users to search the catalog of holdings online.

2005 Mazer begins transition from a completely volunteer-run organization to one with a paid staff. In *In the Life* newsletter, Ann Giagni notes that a regular source of funding, Liberty Hill Foundation, has dried up, and that "Just surviving the next five to ten years will be a major accomplishment. No money from the government. No money from foundations. But women have always done the impossible more often than not with lesbians leading the charge."

2006 Lois Frankel helps the Board of the Mazer lay out a five-year plan.

2007 Mazer forms relationship with UCLA Center for the Study of Women (CSW).

2007 UCLA Center for Community Partnerships awards a two-year Competitive Support for Campus Partners grant to CSW Director Kathleen McHugh and CSW for the "'Access Mazer' Project: Organizing and Digitizing the Lesbian-Feminist Archive in Los Angeles," which processed and digitized several key Los Angeles–themed collections.

2007 Angela Brinskele joins the Board of the Mazer.

2009 UCLA and Mazer celebrate the launch of "The June Mazer Lesbian Archive at UCLA" with a symposium and reception. Speakers include Ann Cvetkovich, T-Kay Sangwand, James Hixon, and Candace Moore.

2009 Last print issue of *In the Life* newsletter published.

2009 Five of the Mazer's collections are made available at the UCLA Library Digital Library: Southern California Women for Understanding; Connexxus/ Centro de Mujeres; Women Against Violence Against Women; Margaret (Peg) Cruikshank Papers; and Lillian Faderman Papers.

2011 CSW and the UCLA Library receives a National Endowment for the Humanities grant for "Making Invisible Histories Visible: Preserving the Legacy of Lesbian Feminist Activism and Writing in Los Angeles," a three-year project to arrange, describe, digitize, and make physically and electronically

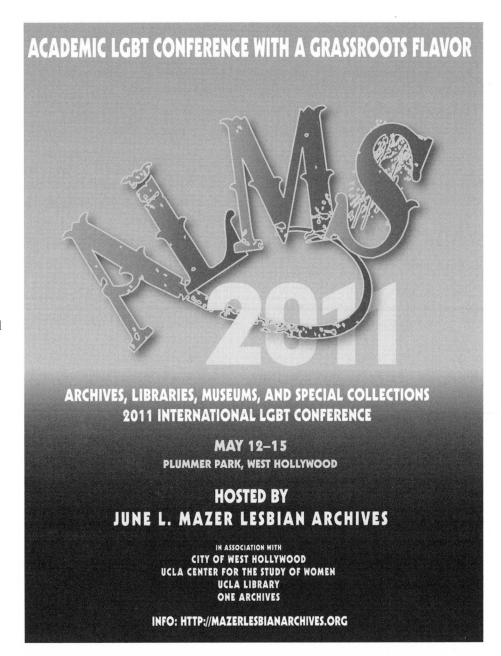

ACADEMIC LGBT CONFERENCE WITH A GRASSROOTS FLAVOR

ALMS 2011

ARCHIVES, LIBRARIES, MUSEUMS, AND SPECIAL COLLECTIONS
2011 INTERNATIONAL LGBT CONFERENCE

MAY 12–15
PLUMMER PARK, WEST HOLLYWOOD

HOSTED BY
JUNE L. MAZER LESBIAN ARCHIVES

IN ASSOCIATION WITH
CITY OF WEST HOLLYWOOD
UCLA CENTER FOR THE STUDY OF WOMEN
UCLA LIBRARY
ONE ARCHIVES

INFO: HTTP://MAZERLESBIANARCHIVES.ORG

accessible two major clusters of Mazer collections related to West Coast lesbian/feminist activism and writing since the 1930s.

2011 Mazer Archives, in conjunction with the City of West Hollywood and CSW, hosts the Third International ALMS (Archives, Libraries, Museums, and Special Collections)

Conference in Plummer Park, West Hollywood.

2012 Colonel Margarethe Cammermeyer donates her personal papers.

About the Contributors

Sandra Brasda is a Ph.D. candidate in the history department at UCLA. She is a gender and culture historian of 1960s America.

Angela Brinskele is a professional photographer and the director of communications for the June L. Mazer Lesbian Archives. She has documented the LGBT community in Southern California through photography with a special emphasis on lesbians for more than twenty-five years.

Julie K. Childers is the founder of JKC Consulting in Philadelphia, PA. Childers was assistant sirector at the Center for the Study of Women from 2010 to 2013. A scholar of U.S. women's social movements, Childers holds a Ph.D. in Sociology from Boston College. Her dissertation research project was a study of the third-wave women's health movement in Boston, MA. She co-founded a research center at the Planned Parenthood League of Massachusetts, bridging clinical and health education research.

Marika Cifor is a doctoral student in the Department of Information Studies with a concentration in Gender Studies at UCLA She received a M.A. in History and an M.S.L.I.S. with a concentration in Archives Management from Simmons College. Her doctoral research concerns the collaborations and partnerships of LGBTQ community archives and more traditional institutional archives from a queer and feminist perspective.

Jonathan Cohn teaches at the University of Alberta and his current research focuses on the discourses of choice and freedom that pervade the history of digital media and technologies. His work has appeared in *Camera Obscura, Spectator,* and several anthologies.

Courtney Dean received her M.L.I.S. from UCLA in 2013. She works as a Project Archivist at the Los Angeles County Museum of Art's Balch Art Research Library.

Angel Diaz is pursuing her M.L.I.S. degree in the Department of Information Studies. In 2013, she received the Harold T. Pinkett Minority Student Award from the Society of American Archivists. She has been involved with several archival community service initiatives that document and preserve the Mexican American experience, including the establishment of the forthcoming Cesar Chavez Archives at the National Chavez Center in Keene, California.

Sharon E. Farb is associate university librarian at UCLA. Farb has worked in the UCLA library since 1989. She has held various positions, including head of digital collections services. She specializes in digital collections management and licensing, intellectual property and copyright management issues, budgetary constraints, and statewide and national consortial initiatives.

Ann Giagni has served as President of the Board of the June L. Mazer Lesbian Archives since 1996. She received her BA from NYU and a Master's degree from USC. She is currently a student at Southwestern Law School. An award-winning theater producer, she had a 31 year career with the City of Los Angeles and ten years as a local labor leader. She has been centrally involved in LGBTQ politics since the 1970s. Her leadership role of the Mazer Archives includes hosting the 2011 International ALMS Conference for LGBTQ Archives, and negotiaing the Deed of Gift and MOU with the UCLA Library that began the relationship between the two organizations.

Lizette Guerra is the archivist and librarian at the UCLA Chicano Studies Research Center Library and Archive. She received an MA in Latin American Studies and an M.L.I.S. in Information Studies from UCLA in 2007. She has research experience working in museums both in Mexico and Guatemala. She has done archival, curatorial, and cataloging work for the Autry National Center's Southwest Museum of the American Indian and the Museum of the American West in Los Angeles, CA.

Molly S. Jacobs is a doctoral candidate in the department of Sociology at UCLA. She is currently working on her dissertation, an analysis of the mobilization of the Mattachine Society and the Daughters of Bilitis and the role they played in the Homophile Movement. When she is not working on her dissertation, Molly is either teaching undergraduates or preventing her daughter from biting other toddlers on the playground. These two tasks are surprisingly similar.

Elizabeth Joffrian is director of Heritage Resources at Western Washington University. She leads the libraries' Special Collections, University Archives and Record Center, and the Center for Pacific Northwest Studies. Joffrion previously was a senior program officer at the National Endowment for the Humanities, Division of Preservation and Access, where she coordinated the Preservation Assistance Grants Program. Before joining NEH in 2006, she was the head archivist at the Center for Pacific Northwest Studies at Western Washington University and affiliated faculty in its graduate program in Archives and Records Management. She has held professional positions at the Smithsonian Institution, North Carolina State Archives and the Historic New Orleans Collection, and has also taught courses on archives and special collections at Catholic University in Washington, DC.

Brenda Johnson-Grau is an editor, designer, and pop music scholar. She has completed more than thirty projects for a range of publishers, including the Smithsonian, UCLA Latin American Institute, Skirball Cultural Center, Rhino Records, and the Cotsen Institute. She has served on the editorial board of *Popular Music and Society* since 1994 and founded *OneTwoThreeFour, a rock and roll quarterly,* which was published between 1984 and 1991. She has been publications manager at Center for the Study of Women since 2006.

Kathleen A. McHugh has been director of Center for the Study of Women since 2005. She is the Co-Principal Investigator—with former UCLA University Librarian Gary Strong—on "Making Invisible Histories Visible: Preserving the Legacy of Feminist Activism and Writing in Los Angeles." For this project, she secured a three year Humanities Collections and Reference Resources (HCRR) grant from the National Endowment of the Humanities. McHugh is a Professor in the Department of English and in the Cinema and Media Studies program of the Department of Film, Television, and Digital Media at UCLA. She has authored *Jane Campion* (University of Illinois Press, 2007) and *American Domesticity: From How-To Manual to Hollywood Melodrama* (Oxford University Press, 1999) and co-edited *South Korean Golden Age Melodrama: Gender, Genre, and National Cinema* (Wayne State University Press, 2005) and a special issue of *SIGNS* on "Film Feminisms."

Archna Patel is a fourth-year undergraduate student at UCLA. She is studying history and art history, and she will be graduating in the spring.

Ben Raphael Sher is a doctoral student in UCLA's Cinema and Media Studies Department. His dissertation is titled "Fraught Pleasures: Domestic Trauma and Cinephilia in American Culture." His writing has appeared in various publications, including *From Madea to Mogul: Critical Perspectives on Tyler Perry* (forthcoming from University of

Mississippi Press), *Leonard Maltin's Movie Guide, Fangoria,* and the website for Chiller TV, a division of NBC Universal. At UCLA, he has taught courses on queer media spectatorship, domestic trauma in American genre films, and media studies pedagogy.

Virginia Steel is university librarian at UCLA. Throughout her career, Steel has focused on understanding the information needs of faculty, students, and staff and enhancing and building services and collections to meet those needs. She has established and fostered strategic partnerships with campus organizations, philanthropists, corporations, and foundations to improve services and support for students and faculty and to provide physical and virtual spaces that foster creativity, engagement, and a wide range of intellectual pursuits.

Michael Stone is archives and digital projects manager at UCLA Chicano Studies Research Center. Previously, he worked at Columbia University at the Butler Library Rare Book and Manuscript Archive. He graduated from Columbia University Film School in 2003.

Daniel Williford is completing his Ph.D. in the Department of English at UCLA. He is an Adjunct Instructor in the Department of Critical Theory and Social Justice at Occidental College in Los Angeles.

Stacy Wood is a graduate student in the M.L.I.S. program at UCLA. Her career interests include library studies, gender and sexuality studies, feminism, youth services, censorship, literacy and community programming, and archiving self- and/or independently published materials.

Index